FINANCIAL RECOVERY

FINANCIAL RECOVERY

Developing a
Healthy Relationship with Money

KAREN McCALL
Foreword by JOHN BRADSHAW

New World Library
Novato, California

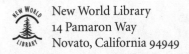 New World Library
14 Pamaron Way
Novato, California 94949

MoneyMinder® is a registered trademark of Karen McCall.

Text design by Tona Pearce Myers

Library of Congress Cataloging-in-Publication Data
McCall, Karen.
 Financial recovery : developing a healthy relationship with money / Karen McCall ; foreword by John Bradshaw.
    p.   cm.
Includes bibliographical references and index.
ISBN 978-1-57731-928-3 (pbk. : alk. paper)
1. Finance, Personal. 2. Money. 3. Finance, Personal—Psychological aspects. 4. Money—Psychological aspects. I. Title.
HG179.M37414 2011
332.024—dc22   2011006703

First printing, May 2011
ISBN 978-1-57731-928-3
Printed in Canada on 100% postconsumer-waste recycled paper

g New World Library is a proud member of the Green Press Initiative.

10 9 8 7 6 5 4 3 2 1

To Frances and Vincent Kreizenbeck:
Aunt Fran and Uncle Binnie, you gave me a home,
you gave me your love, you saved my life.
From the bottom of my heart, I thank you.

To honor the confidentiality of my clients, I have changed names and other identifying details. The essential truths of their circumstances and the insights they gained during their process of Financial Recovery are authentic and reflect the dilemmas and discoveries made by many clients with whom I've worked over the years. In the cases where last names are used, these are professionals who have agreed to share their stories and to be identified.

Contents

Foreword

I am honored to introduce Karen McCall's book *Financial Recovery* to readers. Having experienced severe poverty in my childhood, I lived the next forty-five years compulsively working and catastrophizing about money. By 1979 I was psychologically counseling fifty-plus hours a week, I was giving frequent seminars for one chemical and two oil companies, and I was directing the Palmer Drug Abuse Program in Los Angeles from my home in Houston. In 1980 I was asked to be on the board of directors of Texas General Oil Company, and they appointed me director of human resources.

As with many of the people whose stories Karen shares, my financial problems were about more than just sound money and debt management; they were about the fear that I would never have enough. I would spend rather lavishly at times, but then I would be ravaged by guilt and driven by a feeling of scarcity. I was clearly addicted to making money. One of the central themes of this book is that financial problems stem from an unhealthy relationship with money, and this was certainly the case for me.

In August 1981 I was spending a week in a small cabin that I owned in Minnesota. In those days, I was jogging about five miles a day, four times a week. On the 13th of August I set out on my daily run. I was quite energized, and before I knew it I had run ten miles and was headed toward a little town called Pequot Lakes. I felt high, in what experts on creativity call the "flow." Those who run long distances talk about reaching a state that they describe as an endorphin high. Whatever it is called, I was quite mood-altered. I felt that I could run forever.

As I ran to Pequot Lakes, I looked out at the horizon and saw what seemed to be a cloud formation that outlined the face of Christ. I immediately experienced an auditory intuition that clearly gave me the message, "Do the work that you were intended to do, and your money worries will cease."

I was deeply moved and quite perplexed by the experience. Although I'd had a strong religious upbringing and studied to be a Catholic priest, at that time I was in a serious state of questioning Christianity, and I had not been to church in years.

In my latest book, *Reclaiming Virtue*, I named my experience of jogging on the highway to Pequot Lakes a "grand will" experience. I borrowed this expression from the Jewish philosopher-theologian Martin Buber, who believed that each person has a unique purpose or calling. He believed that when a person makes a choice consistent with their "grand will" (as opposed to their mundane, everyday choices), they are furthering their calling or life purpose.

This is heavy stuff, but it is fully related to the issue of money. The work we do, our life vocation, is the source of income that provides our security, happiness, and freedom. Karen McCall has made the issue of knowing what you need, want, and desire one of the most critical factors in choosing the work you do.

After my "grand will" experience in 1981, I took part in some very serious therapy that helped me grasp many of the things that Karen has learned through her own suffering and has discussed in this book. Chapters 3 and 7 are the real gems for me; they reinforce the insight I gained in my "grand will" experience: that a critical issue in working with and handling money is choosing the work that flows from our "deepest needs and real wants" (what Buddha called "right livelihood"). I found that the work I was "intended to do" was teaching — specifically, to help people grasp the impact of their childhood abandonment, neglect, and abuse wounds and to teach them how to overcome them. In 1984, I filmed a ten-part PBS series called *Bradshaw On: The Family*. These programs showed people the impact of family dysfunction and the tools to heal it. I filmed five more PBS series and wrote six books, one to go with each series. By 1992, I was a millionaire many times over. The strange thing is that from 1985 until now I have stopped thinking, worrying, and catastrophizing about money.

Chapter 3 of this book dovetails beautifully with my work regarding childhood abuse, neglect, and abandonment and the shame that naturally follows. In all the work I've done on this subject, I never fully explored the piece of the puzzle that relates to our money behaviors. Karen has picked up where I left off, illuminating the financial consequences of childhood shame and how we can heal the shame and establish "sterling money behaviors."

The wealthiest and most generous people in our culture share the belief that happiness does not come from the raw accumulation of money. Those who desire to accumulate more and more money are involved in an addictive process — a kind of endless pregnancy that never reaches fruition.

People who have financial success have a healthy relationship with money — the kind of relationship that Karen McCall describes in this timely book. Large numbers of people have money troubles. This book and the Financial Recovery Institute that Karen founded could help these people immensely. After reading this book or attending a Financial Recovery seminar, you will quickly realize that you can transform your creative energy into security and financial freedom.

I urge you to give yourself the gift of reading this book and discovering the road map Karen presents. I would not say that Financial Recovery will necessarily make you a millionaire, and Karen is not promising that either. Being a millionaire does not guarantee financial happiness; achieving true happiness is about much more than making masses of money. Karen's book will show you how making money and enjoying healthy relationships go hand in hand.

— John Bradshaw, bestselling author of
Reclaiming Virtue and *Healing the Shame That Binds You*

The Bridge to a Healthy Relationship with Money

Twenty-seven years ago, I lived at a prestigious address in the exclusive neighborhood of Pacific Heights near the Golden Gate Bridge in San Francisco. I'd begin my days by getting dressed in an elegant suit. Then I'd grab my fine Italian leather briefcase, hop into my silver Nissan 280ZX sports coupe, and head to 101 California Street, an architecturally acclaimed cylindrical glass skyscraper towering over the financial district. Each morning, I stopped at the little café in the lobby to buy a caffe latte before boarding the elevator that would take me to my corner office on the thirty-first floor with its spectacular view of San Francisco Bay.

If you'd seen me then, you may have thought, "Wow, what a success!" But, as we know, appearances can be deceiving. You wouldn't have seen what I was hiding behind the impressive facade — a secret, a dirty little secret. The truth was that I was flat broke. Bill collectors were hounding me. I had no savings. I was driving with an expired license and past-due registration. I was behind on my rent and car payments. And things were steadily getting worse. In short, I was in a financial mess.

How could things have gotten so bad?

I had been married — twice. On the heels of my second divorce two years earlier, I began running through my savings at a rapid pace. When we split up, my ex-husband and I sold the home that we'd built together. This, in combination with my divorce settlement meant that I was able to put a tidy sum in the bank. This could have lasted quite a while if I'd understood anything about my relationship with money. But I wasn't in touch with reality — or with the internal forces that drove me. My kids were in college, and it was the first time in my life that I was alone. I felt afraid and lonely. My solution was to get away. I moved to California's spectacular Mendocino coast, where I adopted a grandiose lifestyle, inviting my city friends up for weekends of lavish meals and drinks.

Within a short time, I shot through all my money. Credit was never easier to get than in the 1980s, and I signed on without hesitation. My assets evaporated and my debts mounted. When my money was gone, I took a job as a salesperson for a large computer company and moved to a studio apartment near San Francisco's Ghirardelli Square. Every day I would come home and toss my bills into a deep wooden bowl on top of my refrigerator — then ignore them. The bowl held dozens of unopened bills, including several notices from the IRS. I was in a hole and quickly digging my way deeper and deeper. It was scary to be behind on my bills, but I was too embarrassed to reach out for help. Surely, everyone else understood money and I would look foolish. I didn't have the first clue about how to handle my money troubles. I didn't want to think about the impending disaster, so I avoided the bowl in my kitchen. But there was no money left, and the bowl on the fridge was overflowing.

No one in my life guessed that I was on the verge of financial ruin except my friend Tom Johnson. We didn't speak about it directly, but he started showing up at my door with self-help audiocassettes. One night I found myself in a state of debilitating fear. I had gotten an eviction notice. With the pressure building, I reached for one of those tapes, a program called *Move Ahead with Possibility Thinking* by Robert H. Schuller. Schuller's words of hope and encouragement were a balm to my fears. Listening to the message, I felt uplifted and energized to take action. "Once you act," he said, "more possibilities will open up for you."[1]

I opened my mind to possibility thinking and mustered the courage to drag the big bowl down from the refrigerator. I sat at my kitchen table and opened every bill. I then made a list of what I owed. Though it was scary to finally see the total of all my bills, there was also a sense of relief that came with finally looking at the reality of my financial circumstances. One thing was certain: I could no longer live the way I'd been living. Something had to change, and change fast.

That was my wake-up call. I realized it would be impossible for me to pay both rent and a car payment. Something had to go. Because I was in sales, my car was key to my livelihood, so the choice seemed obvious. I was too ashamed to tell my family about my predicament, so I had to do something to come up with some money quickly, and I had to find a free place to live. Otherwise, I'd soon find myself on the street. I picked up the *San Francisco Chronicle* and found an ad that read: "Professional couple in Pacific Heights seeks cook to prepare meals five nights a week in exchange for room and board."

When I interviewed with the older couple who'd placed the ad, they were curious as to why I'd want to be their live-in cook when I already had a good job in the financial district. I couldn't be truthful and reveal that I was desperate for a place to live. Instead, I said that moving in with them would be a smart way to build up my cash reserves. When they hired me on the spot, an enormous sense of relief washed over me.

That Saturday, I held a sale in the courtyard of my apartment building and sold everything I owned. Forty years of precious possessions and irreplaceable mementos were gone in an afternoon for pennies on the dollar. It was a desperate move but the only one I could imagine at the time. It was emotionally devastating. I arrived at my new position as live-in cook with all my belongings — which now fit in one very small car.

Now, at the end of every day — after leaving my bay-view office, hopping into my shiny sports car, and driving to a Pacific Heights mansion — I would arrive at the maid's quarters. I would change out of my business suit and put on an apron before heading for the kitchen. My co-workers surely would have been stunned. Though I had dodged the immediate bullet, a long-standing sense of shame soon began to erode my temporary feeling of triumph.

You would think that the new living arrangement would have solved my immediate problem, but it didn't. I had been living in a "money coma," completely unconscious of my finances until desperate circumstances had finally roused me. I had to develop a new relationship with money. I had to learn some basic, practical skills about how to manage money. I had to discover what had led to my problems so that I wouldn't find myself in this situation ever again.

FINANCIAL RECOVERY IS BORN

In working through my issues with money, I soon found out that there were no services for people like me. There was a gap — a *huge* gap into which millions of people just like me were falling. On one side, there were financial planners, advisers, and accountants to help people who had money, and on the other side, there were credit counselors offering minimal support with strict budgeting plans for those who didn't. I wasn't a candidate for either. Neither service addressed my pain, sense of deprivation, shame, and fears or could help me gain an understanding of how my history had fueled such harmful choices about money. They could not guide me on the inner journey I needed to take.

There was some help out there, though, and I found it when I accidentally stumbled into a Debtors Anonymous (DA) meeting, a free self-help program. Oh, the relief that came over me when I heard people openly talking about their money problems and realized I wasn't alone! I could come out of hiding! By attending meetings, I began to emerge from my secrecy and isolation; I knew for the first time that there were countless other people like me and I could give up the struggle and shame of the life I'd been leading. It helped me look at my pattern of "debting" and overspending. In addition to attending DA meetings, I continued listening to inspirational tapes that kept me focused on possibilities and taking one day at a time.

I started taking simple steps that were amazingly powerful. By creating a set of simple worksheets and easy money-tracking tools unlike any I'd found, I put myself on a new financial path. Empowered by these tools and the strategies and insights I'd been acquiring, I quickly began to see results, experiencing not only more financial stability but also a greater sense of well-being. The vision of a future beyond my immediate state of devastation started to come into focus. It was an image of the life I actually wanted to live.

Eventually, I began to think of what I was developing as a personal recovery process — Financial Recovery. This period of my life and all that I was learning felt like an extraordinary experience of grace. I was so excited and grateful for the relief I felt that I wanted to share what I'd discovered. In what has since emerged as my life's work, I began teaching Financial Recovery to all those around me who were suffering in the same way I had been.

In 1988 I started my business and named it Financial Recovery, which later became the Financial Recovery Institute. My goal was to provide counseling to individuals, couples, and business owners wanting to gain clarity about and improve their money situation. I worked with people of all income levels and walks of life in a powerful process that immediately began to transform behavior and over time changed their entire financial lives. I've heard hundreds of stories from all sorts of clients and trainees. The universal desire among all my clients was to understand their relationship with money.

Since then I've been working side by side with clients to help them figure out what Financial Recovery means for them. I'll never forget one of my early clients, a building contractor. He arrived at our first session carrying two five-gallon plastic paint buckets chock-full of the bills and paperwork that he said he simply could not manage. This man knew he couldn't do it alone. He was handing it over, asking for help, and I knew the Financial Recovery process could help him.

I've seen people nearly broken by their financial worries, suffering ill health, fractured relationships, and an underlying sense of panic and shame that permeated every aspect of their lives. I've counseled clients with fortunes who were unable to feel secure, with their family relationships all tangled up in the strings of wealth. Financial circumstances often made them feel unable to take care of their most basic needs and those of their families. Like me, most of those people felt embarrassed and ashamed by not being able to manage their financial lives. This has taught me that everyone, whether they have a lot of money or a little, deserves support and compassion to improve their relationship with money.

I've watched people journey from despair, shame, and hopelessness to hope, self-esteem, and abundance as I've guided them through the stages of Financial Recovery. This program has been acknowledged and embraced by experts in both the financial and mental health professions. But what continues to be rewarding to me is seeing how it helps people. Whether they come from inherited wealth or have struggled with debt their whole lives, people from all kinds of financial circumstances have transformed their lives by using this process.

FULL CIRCLE

I emailed the final version of this manuscript to my publisher on July 5, 2010. To celebrate the completion of the book and my sixty-seventh birthday, I treated myself to a three-day stay at Cavallo Point, a former U.S. Army post that has been converted into a lodge, restaurant, and cooking school. Described in its brochure as a "view with rooms," the Sausalito resort overlooks San Francisco Bay, with a spectacular view of the Golden Gate Bridge. After attending a fabulous Saturday evening cooking class (and enjoying the meal we'd prepared), I stepped outside to take in my surroundings. In the distance was the twinkling skyline of San Francisco and, to the west, the magnificent Golden Gate Bridge, blanketed in a thin layer of fog. I smelled the salt water and felt the drizzle of fog on my skin. I felt exhilarated and overcome with a feeling of gratitude. Looking ahead to the beginning of my sixty-eighth year, I imagined all kinds of new possibilities.

As I stood looking across the gray waters of the bay, appreciating my life, my mind traveled back to twenty-seven years ago, when creditors were hounding me and I was facing eviction. I had no idea how I was going to meet my most basic needs. One day, I felt the walls closing in on me. I simply had to get out of my apartment for a short breather. I got in my car and drove with no particular destination in mind. I found myself at Fort Mason, under the Golden Gate, looking toward Sausalito. As I stood there on the rocky shore, the most amazing thought came to me. *This is so incredibly beautiful, and it's free — this can never be taken away from me!* I knew in that moment that no matter what my financial circumstances were, I could find inspiration and renewal. I'd been so deep in despair that it felt like a miracle that my spirit could be so uplifted. With those thoughts, I felt a powerful surge of energy, inspiration, and courage.

Nothing about my circumstances had changed, yet somehow *everything* had changed. Deep down, I knew I would find the way. I didn't realize it then, but what I now know is that courage came from a connection with a power much greater than myself. This power has always been there for me, even in my darkest moments. I had found the bridge that would take me from where I was then to where I wanted to be, and I crossed that bridge one step at a time.

As I stood there on the opposite shore all these years later, reliving that extraordinary moment from the past, I realized I had come full circle. This iconic structure, the Golden Gate Bridge, had become symbolic of my life's journey. I reflected that I'd been walking, one step at a time, across my own bridge — the bridge of Financial Recovery. I had been given a golden opportunity to help others step into their own Financial Recovery and journey across their own bridges.

I hope that in some small way my experience of Financial Recovery and the stories I'll share in these pages will give you the hope and courage you need to find your own "Golden Gate."

WHAT FINANCIAL RECOVERY IS NOT

Financial Recovery is not about the latest moneymaking trend or the hottest investment. I don't promise an easy, pain-free way to become a millionaire while you sleep or to pay off your mortgage in one year. For many of us, just getting more money will not solve all our problems, especially if there are deeper issues. More money often merely adds more zeroes at the end of financial problems without solving them at all.

Financial Recovery is not a one-time quick fix for financial woes, nor is it a traditional budget-planning tool or quick get-out-of-debt repayment plan. Though these may be temporary fixes, they are not sustainable over time. They don't address the core causes of troubling financial patterns, attitudes, and behaviors one has and needs to change to maintain a healthier lifestyle. We need not only practical tools but also insight. Together, they can help us to both manage the sometimes overwhelming feelings that arise when we attempt to change our relationship with money and keep self-defeating cycles from recurring.

WHAT EXACTLY *IS* FINANCIAL RECOVERY? AND WHAT DOES IT MEAN FOR YOU?

Financial Recovery is a process that helps you to develop a healthy relationship with money that is both healing and life-changing. It enables you to understand *where* you are, *how* you got there, how to *change* your financial circumstances in the present, and how to *maintain* a healthy financial way of life long into the future. Financial Recovery simultaneously addresses your internal needs and your external behaviors, because these must be in harmony with each other

Financial Recovery is a fundamental shift in the way you understand and behave around money. It involves practical steps for managing your money wisely. It is ideal for young parents wondering how they're going to provide for their family's future and pay the monthly bills. It's also for seniors on fixed incomes trying to make ends meet. It's for small-business owners worrying about covering their overhead. Financial Recovery can help those from affluent backgrounds who may have mixed feelings about an inheritance or trust fund, or who may want to break away from dependence on family money. It's for young people starting out on their career path and wanting to do it right. And it's for individuals who have maxed out their credit cards. Additionally, it's for people who choose a life of voluntary simplicity and, in these tough economic times, for the millions of people who have been forced into a lifestyle of *involuntary* simplicity. Financial Recovery can be helpful to those who have been dealt pay cuts or lost their jobs or even their homes.

By practicing the skills you will learn in this process, you will come to identify, understand, and change the attitudes and beliefs that have led to your pattern of financial distress — whether it's a recent problem or one that has plagued you for a lifetime. You will understand how "money mindfulness" can work for you, building your awareness and strengthening your financial health. You'll learn how to save your way out of debt without living in a state of deprivation. By distinguishing your deepest, most genuine needs from the inadequate ways you've tried to meet them, you'll create a livable spending plan that allows you to feel fulfilled while simultaneously meeting your goals.

It's not about how to get more "stuff"; it's about how to benefit from more of the *right stuff*: people, experiences, and things that nourish you on every level of your being, bringing you joy and satisfaction. Through Financial Recovery you will become the designer of your own financial life as *you* define it. With small steps, you'll begin to see large changes in your financial life.

Your situation may not be as extreme as mine was. Or yours may be worse. Either way, Financial Recovery will teach you skills that will always be available to you for reaching any financial goal. It will also continue to help you as you achieve greater levels of success and stability.

If you are feeling uneasy about your relationship with money for any reason — even if you can't name it — Financial Recovery will help you create the life you want. Free from shame and worry about money, you can devote your energies to the things that matter most to you: family, friendships, creative endeavors, intellectual pursuits, spiritual practices, or whatever interests provide enjoyment, fulfillment, and satisfaction. Financial Recovery allows you to be the supreme choice maker in your own life.

Imagine the possibilities!

THE STEPS ACROSS THE BRIDGE

Each of the eight chapters of this book presents a key element of the Financial Recovery process. Chapter 1 starts you out on your journey of healing by asking you to examine your relationship with money. You'll explore the various types of what I call "financial dis-ease," including elements of obsession, shame, secrecy, denial, lack of control, and the inability to change patterns despite dire consequences. Becoming aware of your relationship with money is the first step on the road to Financial Recovery.

Chapter 2 explores how people get stuck in the same old money troubles over and over again — what I call the Money/ Life Drain, a vicious cycle that erodes not only our financial lives but the emotional, social, and spiritual qualities we want out of life too. But don't worry — you'll also learn the fail-safe steps for getting out of the Money/Life Drain.

In chapter 3, we'll explore the crucial difference between needs and wants. Much of what puts us at risk for entering the dangerous waters of the Money/Life Drain is an inability to understand our deepest needs, wants, and desires. This leads us to spend money in ways that leave our needs unmet and drive us to spend even more. Getting in touch with what is really important to you is a major part of designing a financial life that is stable and fulfilling.

In chapter 4, we'll get into the nuts and bolts of Financial Recovery. You'll learn tracking, the tool for becoming conscious of and connected to your money behaviors so that you can emerge from the financial fog — or worse, a money coma — and have the financial life you choose. Your growing understanding of your wants and needs will be invaluable as you begin this process. You'll learn to track your spending, an integral part of the Financial Recovery process.

Chapter 5 addresses the heart of Financial Recovery: creating your individual spending plan. This is the part that I get really excited about. Planning is what gives Financial Recovery its power. This chapter will help you to experience the real freedoms of creating your individual plan. This is not just the age-old budget — not just an exercise in numbers. Designing a spending plan, your plan, based on your needs, gives you the freedom of knowing ahead of time that you can not only make it through the month but design the life you want to live.

In chapter 6, we'll talk about a strategy that makes Financial Recovery different from other programs. By understanding the powerful interaction between saving and debt, you'll learn the high-impact strategy of "Saving Your Way Out of Debt." People get out of debt all the time. In this chapter you'll learn not only how to get out of debt but how to stay out of debt as well. I believe you should get to take care of yourself, enjoy life, and not put your whole life on hold while you're repaying debt. That's what makes Financial Recovery a sustainable way of life. The tried-and-true strategies I suggest will help you to crush debt before it crushes you. If debt is not a big issue for you, the information in this chapter might keep it from becoming an issue down the road.

In chapter 7, we'll look at the tightly interlocked issues of work and money. Financial Recovery is about creating the life you want, and your work is a huge part of that life. You'll examine your belief systems and attitudes about earning or not earning enough money to have the life you want. Having that understanding empowers you to make choices about the work you want to do and the money you want to earn.

Chapter 8 is where we explore living expansively: moving from shaky to stable, and from stable to what I call "sterling money behaviors." It's exciting to experience the transformation that comes with achieving and maintaining a financial life that is not only stable but deeply fulfilling. Amazingly, this process offers even more to enrich your life. A deeper level of transformation takes place when you adopt sterling money behaviors. The last chapter will help you define these for yourself.

Throughout the book you'll find practical exercises that will help you get a clear picture of your financial life and the motivations and tendencies that have led you to this point. In many places, I ask you to write down the answers to questions about your relationship with money. And I invite you to jot down your reflections whenever they come up. To prepare yourself for this, you will need a money journal. It can be a simple inexpensive notebook or something more special; all that matters is that you feel good writing in it. Take note of your thoughts and feelings as you explore your changing relationship with money. Journaling has proved an invaluable, eye-opening part of the Financial Recovery process.

The process as a whole has benefited thousands over the past twenty years. People who have spent years, even decades, struggling just to make it through the month have found that they can achieve a sense of financial well-being that they'd never thought possible. People have found an expansive financial life and profound fulfillment that extends far beyond money.

While the journey of Financial Recovery requires commitment, the steps are fairly simple, and the rest of this book will guide you. I invite you now, as I've invited so many clients at the beginning of their journeys, to take your first steps on the bridge to your own healthy relationship with money.

CHAPTER ONE

Understanding Your Relationship with Money

Getting to the Root of the Problem

> At the moment of commitment,
> the universe conspires to assist you.
>
> — **BARBRA STREISAND**

You picked up this book, so chances are you're feeling some concern or discomfort around your financial life, be it a sense of instability, chronic unmanageability, or simply a lack of knowledge about your finances. Maybe you're worried about your future or struggling just to make it month to month. Have you been plagued with money problems for years? Are you watching your resources dwindle? Have you tried countless times to figure your way out of your financial mess, only to find yourself in it over and over again? Are your worries about money occupying more of your energy than feels comfortable? Are you keeping financial secrets, afraid of the shame you'll feel if they're discovered? Do you argue about money with your loved ones? Is your health, emotional well-being, or quality of life compromised by your concerns about money? Are you just sick of living on the edge?

If you answer yes to one or more of these questions — and you're willing to commit to a process that will fundamentally change your relationship with money — you're ready to begin your own Financial Recovery.

This process has brought transformation to my life and to the lives of those who have embraced it. You've likely tried many things to improve your situation and stabilize your spending or debt. People who have tried and failed in other attempts to change their money behaviors have found the practical and emotional support they need in Financial Recovery.

Many people hit rock bottom in their relationship with money before getting help. They feel desperate and unable to figure out how to change their financial circumstances. But you don't have to wait to reverse the downward spiral and begin your process of Financial Recovery. No matter how severe your money issues are, you can reverse course and move toward a healthier relationship with money, starting today.

There came a moment for me, as there is for so many who struggle in their relationship with money, when I could no longer deny that I'd been overcome by the consequences of my financial behaviors. I realized that every attempt I'd made to fix my financial troubles and change my money behaviors had failed. Something had to change, and that something was me. I had to look at all I'd been avoiding and let go of the fantasy that I could manage things. Everything I'd been tolerating — the stress, the obsessing, the worrying, the secrecy — all became intolerable. I felt broken, isolated, alone, and ashamed. Emotionally exhausted and spiritually depleted, I had to recognize the truth. I had to let go of the illusion that I could think my way out of this problem, that I could figure it out.

Freedom comes when we reach a place of admitting that our

best efforts and sincerest intentions haven't worked to improve our financial lives. Many of us find ourselves in a troubling relationship with money, lacking the skills and tools for good money management and underestimating the emotional aspects of what may be driving our behaviors with money. This is when a freeing realization sets in: *I can't do this on my own.*

If you're someone who has struggled in your relationship with money, I'll say to you what I say to clients: "It doesn't ever have to be this bad again." Your financial life can begin to improve right now, right here, with the information and ideas you'll get from these pages. You can begin Financial Recovery right this minute.

The Root of the Problem

Most people assume that not having enough money is the cause of their financial struggles. While "not enough" can sometimes be a problem, it is often not the primary problem. At the root of many, if not most, people's ongoing financial trouble is an unhealthy relationship with money.

When I started to counsel people in the Financial Recovery process, I assumed that clients would come to me wanting simple debt repayment plans or advice on spending and saving — basically, *information* about money. But I discovered over time that the vast majority of my clients knew that it was not just information they needed. They wanted to understand their *relationship with money* and make lasting changes. People with ongoing financial challenges, cyclic patterns, and recurring money dramas usually understand that their problems with money have little to do with math — they're about their relationship with money.

Joe and Valerie knew they had to change their relationship with money.

CASE STUDY
Joe and Valerie

Joe was a young professional. He and his wife, Valerie, came to see me shortly after the birth of their first child. Joe had been struggling for years with credit card debt. Like many of us, Joe felt ashamed. He had kept his debt a dark secret, even from those closest to him.

He had tears in his eyes as he told me his reason for coming: "When I held my baby in my arms for the first time, I realized that unless I did something different, a day would soon come when he might want a new bike or to go to a summer camp, and I wouldn't be able to provide it. Not because I didn't make enough money but because of the financial mess I've created. I have to do something."

I assured Joe that by starting this process now and continuing the work going forward, he would be able to provide for his family. He and Valerie started working with the Financial Recovery program to address the problems of how they were relating to their money. They developed skills and practices to make it part of their lives. Joe recently called me. It had been several years since I had last seen him. He wanted to tell me all about the trip he had just taken with his son — a trip to Disneyland paid for with savings. In the past he would have used credit cards for such a trip, a practice that would compromise the future he and Valerie wanted to build for their family. It was touching to hear the sense of freedom and pride in his voice.

Joe and Valerie did not have to lose everything to become willing to change their relationship with money. For others, this realization comes only after things have gotten much worse.

Some people, such as Julia, become so overwhelmed by money problems that they put their lives at risk.

CASE STUDY
Julia

Early in my practice I had a client named Julia. As Julia was driving one day, her mind was focused on the numbers she was running in her head. She added up the costs of the bills she had to pay and the things she wanted to buy — only to get confused and start the process again several times. Engrossed by the numbers, Julia didn't realize she'd run a red light until a police officer pulled her over. This was her second ticket in the same day, and for the same reason. "I was completely out of my body," she explained. Her preoccupation with money troubles could have killed her.

Julia spent hours obsessing over her finances. "I feel worn out from trying to figure out how to pay for everything each month," she said during our first meeting. "I've tried doing budgets. I've tried putting money in different envelopes, that sort of thing. A couple of times in desperation I put a check in the mail unsigned so that it would have to be returned — just to buy myself some time. My brain is eaten up with bargaining, excuses, and panic. I spend my days feeling angry and ashamed. I'm exhausted."

Stories like Julia's and Joe and Valerie's are fairly common among people who are struggling in their relationship with money. You might be thinking, "I can't have a relationship with money. It's just there. Money is just a thing," or, "I don't even want to think about money, much less have a relationship with it!"

For many of us, our relationship with money is similar to

the one we have with our car: we don't really want to understand
what's going on under the hood; we just want it to work and take
us where we want to go without any trouble. And hey, we're realistic. We know the car needs gas. We realize we have to put a little
fuel and care into the thing, but beyond that we don't want to
hassle with it. That's our wish with money too.

Others want money to be like Santa Claus, a benevolent force
that asks nothing of us but still shows up with a bagful of goodies.
We want money to appear when we want it and need it, to grant
our desires, get us out of trouble, and take care of us.

I understand and have felt this way too. I once thought my
trouble with money was that I simply didn't have enough of
it. That was true in my childhood and young adulthood. *More*
would certainly fix things, I thought. I felt empty and deprived
when I had nothing. Then, when I got money, I ended up spending it recklessly and still felt empty and deprived. This behavior
said a lot more about my relationship with money than about
how much of it I had.

It has become clear to me that absolutely everyone has a relationship with money — whether they want to or not, and whether
they know it or not. The relationship may be harmonious or it
may be acrimonious, distant or obsessive. It may be conscious or
unconscious, supportive or abusive. Undeniably, money is part
of our lives. Every time we earn money, spend it, borrow it, save
it, win it, or lose it, we are relating to it, ascribing meaning to it,
and deriving meaning from it. Money affects how we live, our
relationships with others, our community, and the world.

The meaning we attribute to money largely determines our
relationship with it and results from all our personal history, culture, and experience. If I were to interview ten people, money
would likely mean completely different things to each of them:

freedom, security, importance, accomplishment, self-esteem, adventure, sex appeal, and so on.

In his book *The Secret Language of Money*, my friend and colleague David Krueger describes our relationship with money as the "longest-running relationship in our life."[1] Even before we are born, our parents' financial circumstances and attitudes lay the groundwork for our first experiences of the world, influencing what kind of prenatal care our mothers receive and what our resources, education, and opportunities will be as we grow. Similarly, after we die, our estate (or lack thereof) lives on. Our children will likely be influenced throughout their lives — consciously or not — by whatever we teach them, intentionally or unintentionally, about money. They may then pass on those lessons to their children, giving our relationship with money a multigenerational impact.

I'm not implying that money is the most important thing in life, and certainly it's not more important than the people we hold dear. Interestingly, though, the healthier your relationship with money, the less likely it is that money will distract you from the things you value most. But money, and our relationship with it, is an undeniable force. Ignoring it doesn't change that. In fact, when we choose to be ostrichlike in our relationship with our finances, hiding our heads in the sand, money exerts an even greater, and usually more negative, influence on us.

Money colors so many areas of our lives — health, education, lifestyle, career, family, self-image, political influence, and so on. Doesn't it make sense to have as healthy a relationship with it as possible?

Situational Problem or Unhealthy Pattern?

Anyone can have a bad romance, and even solid, healthy relationships have their rocky moments. But when someone has a long

string of disastrous romances, it becomes obvious that the situation is attributable not to a particular choice but to a pattern of
choices. The same is true in our relationships with money. Anyone can have a situational financial problem due to extenuating
circumstances — a job loss, a failed business, a medical condition.
But when money issues crop up over and over, or when the same
financial predicament only grows more and more destructive, an
unhealthy pattern of behavior with money exists; our financial
challenges are not merely situational but reflect an ongoing pattern in our relationships with money.

Many major aspects of our lives have an element of recur-
rence. We tend to have the same old arguments over and over
with our loved ones. We always seem to sit in the same chair
at the dinner table. Humans are creatures of habit. This is fine
when the habit is benign, such as misplacing our reading glasses
around the house. But when some patterns become entrenched
— repeated so often that they seem unchangeable — and are actually harmful to our best interest, they can be the source of great
unhappiness and even self-destruction.

This chapter, and indeed this whole book, asks you to open
your mind to new ways of looking at yourself and the patterns,
behaviors, and consequences you experience in your relationship
with money. But be cautious here. We'd all prefer to think that
our money problems are attributable to a series of situations outside our control. But if we're honest with ourselves and accept
that those situations are really part of a larger pattern, we have to
probe to uncover the source of the problem. It's not always easy
to look at our own role in a troubled relationship. By doing so
in your relationship with money, you'll not only become aware
of your patterns but also empower yourself to make the real and
lasting changes that promote balance and financial wellness.

In some cases, financial troubles truly are attributable to outside circumstances. Since the U.S. economic downturn of 2008, people who had been living financially responsible lives, doing all the right things and planning for the future, have found themselves in financial trouble that no one could have anticipated. Disasters, both natural and manmade, have combined with the troubled national economy to launch a relentless barrage on people's financial and emotional lives.

Many people nearing retirement age have watched in horror as their savings have plummeted with the stock and real estate markets. With their funds depleted and little time to recoup, they are facing retirement lives quite different from those they imagined and worked toward. Suddenly, these people must scale back on expenditures they have long taken for granted. They are now forced to design a new financial life, which my friend and colleague Mikelann Valterra, the author of *Why Women Earn Less*, has termed "involuntary simplicity."[2] This refers to the cost-cutting and budgeting measures that their new financial realities necessitate. Fortunately, Financial Recovery can provide solutions for those whose financial difficulties have resulted from circumstances beyond their control as well as for those whose choices and behaviors have led to financial crisis.

However, a financial crisis (even on a national scale) can serve as a magnifying glass focused on those whose relationship with money was unhealthy to start with. For those who have been living on the edge, especially those who have been living that way for a very long time, the recession was not an isolated episode. It was just one more in a long series of events that dragged them down into the enormous pull of something I call the "Money/ Life Drain," which we'll talk more about in chapter 2. It pays to step back from our current financial difficulties and examine what may be more than a situational money problem and instead is a long-standing pattern of money behaviors.

A WORD ABOUT COMPASSION

Before we start examining the various kinds of dysfunctional relationships with money, I invite you to view those who suffer them without judgment or blame. It's easy to look with criticism at those who have spent themselves into crises or whose repeated patterns have caused them and their families harm. It's hard for some people to understand why others live beyond their means, and it's especially easy to judge those who have trust funds or inherited wealth. But I can tell you that those in financial crisis — however they got there — arrive with an abundance of self-judgment. Their self-recrimination, shame, and embarrassment often keep them from seeking help, only making the problems worse. They are in pain and trying to figure out how to make their relationship with money better. But to reach out for help takes guts.

The expression "You're only as sick as your secrets" fittingly describes those in financial crisis. These people often feel embarrassed about their financial circumstances and the behaviors that got them there. When they become willing to come out of their isolation and secrecy, confiding in someone who can help, they begin to show signs of enormous relief. I get very excited when I see the "hope light" come on for people.

Financial Recovery involves taking personal responsibility, and we have to look at our own choices, frailties, patterns, and blind spots in order to enter into this process. It requires honest, clear-eyed self-examination. It requires that we learn skills and tools to manage our money and put what we learn into action. I deeply admire the courage it takes to tackle the work of Financial Recovery.

Most of all, I invite you to suspend the cruelest judgment —

your judgment of yourself. Even if your financial life is a mess, even if you've blown it a dozen times or more or have veered into questionable behavior out of desperation, you can begin your healing process now. You won't improve things by flogging yourself with shame and criticism. That may have been a big part of how the problem got started in the first place. Be kind to yourself. Let yourself learn. Let yourself grow.

Maya Angelou said, "You did then what you knew how to do and when you knew better you did better."[3] That's all we're capable of — doing better than

> *Always do what you are afraid to do.*
> — RALPH WALDO EMERSON

we've done before. We can do this only if we're allowed to learn what we don't yet know. This is what Financial Recovery has taught me and what it can teach you.

FINANCIAL DIS-EASE AND ITS SYMPTOMS

Logically, if one is in need of recovery, then one must suffer from some sort of malady, or *disease*. This word can come loaded with assumptions. Let's look at its most basic definition from *Merriam-Webster's Ninth New Collegiate Dictionary*: "disease, *n.* 1: Trouble. 2: A condition of the living animal or plant body or of one of its parts that impairs the performance of a vital function 3: Harmful development."[4]

Two things have become clear to me, first in my own life, then in my work as a financial counselor. First, because money touches nearly every area of our lives, having a troubled ongoing relationship with it is harmful to our most crucial functioning. Second, the ability to develop a healthy relationship with money requires personal investment and commitment to going forward. This is not so very different from someone changing her diet after being diagnosed with diabetes, or altering his lifestyle after suffering a heart attack.

I have come to regard the emotional stress, compromised relationships, and destructive patterns that many people have with money as financial *dis-ease*. Notice the hyphen. Clearly, if you are in financial trouble, you are not *at ease*. Financial disease can erode relationships with friends, family members, and professional associates. It can also pollute careers, limit creativity, tarnish integrity, and actually be life threatening. How? By causing stress-related illness, neglected medical care, and, in the most dramatic cases, suicide.

To me, the difference between *disease* and *dis-ease* is a simple one. Treating a physical disease usually requires a medical license and is best done by someone other than oneself. But the only person who can identify your financial dis-ease is you. Someone on the outside might not even know you're struggling. With the right tools and support, coupled with a willingness to look honestly at your circumstances, you'll know when you're feeling the pain and symptoms of financial dis-ease. And the remedy is Financial Recovery.

If you suffer from financial dis-ease or behave in compulsive ways with regard to money, it won't just go away. You have to ask for help and accept the fact that you're out of control. You must create and maintain a healthy relationship with money. This is doable but far more complicated than it might sound. Making significant and lasting behavioral changes is an "inside job," and these are usually the toughest kind. Fortunately, this book will arm you with the tools you need.

If you're in a state of financial dis-ease, you've likely experienced one or more of the following symptoms:

Denial

I was in complete denial, throwing my bills into a deep, dark wooden bowl, pretending that the problem was not growing.

Some people have no idea how much money they have, how much they need, or how much they owe. They live in a state of continual vagueness. They don't know where they are financially and have no idea where they're heading. They tell themselves that something will come along to make things better.

Secrecy and Shame

Many times when we're struggling with money, we don't want others to know about it. Perhaps we're afraid people will judge us for not being able to manage things. Or maybe we don't want to look as though we're failing. Sometimes we're spending in ways that we know are destructive, and we don't want to admit this to others, or to ourselves. All of this leads to a vicious cycle of secrecy and shame, with one perpetuating the other. The worst part of living this way is that by trying to hide our problems, we often isolate ourselves from the people and resources that could actually be of help. The more isolated we become, the worse things can get.

Obsession

Many people struggling with money find themselves obsessed with trying to figure out the problem. They run numbers constantly in their heads; they calculate money on the backs of envelopes, trying to figure a way to manage what has become unmanageable. Others spend hours scheming about the things they want to purchase. They're unable to calm their thoughts, and it disturbs their sleep. No matter what they're doing, their minds are elsewhere, thinking about money: how they're going to get it, how they'll spend it, or how they need to juggle it. Worries about money take up the emotional and mental space that was once devoted to enjoying life and being with loved ones.

Lack of Control

When someone has lost control over money behaviors, she may start every day with the best intentions. She promises herself that her spending will change. She goes to Macy's vowing she'll buy just one blouse but leaves with four. She intends to pay cash for everything but ends up using her credit card again and again. Earnest intentions to save money or pay bills on time disappear each month like so much dust in a strong wind. Each day, she makes the promise again: "Today will be different." But every day ends up just like the one before.

Inability to Change Behavior Despite Negative Consequences

Faced with the consequences of our money behaviors, we tell ourselves, "Never again." We never want to have to tell our loved ones that we're in a financial jam — again. We can't stand the stress, the worry, the sweat-producing anxiety. We want no more of the shame that results when we have neglected a financial responsibility or broken another promise or told another half-truth. But somehow our old ways of spending, or avoiding, or deceiving, resume despite all the pain we want to avoid. Though we tell ourselves it will be different this time, we soon find ourselves on a well-worn path — the same path we promised never to walk again.

THE SYMPTOMS OF FINANCIAL DIS-EASE listed above can also be symptoms of other compulsive behaviors. People with unhealthy relationships with money often experience the same types of emotional turmoil as those with other kinds of addictions. For those who struggle with their relationship with money, the path of healing is Financial Recovery.

The First Steps: Assessing Where You Are Now and Where You Want to Go

Sometimes getting started is the toughest step of all. I encourage my clients, and now I'll encourage you, to approach the process with what Buddhists call "beginner's mind."

When my oldest grandson, Mathieu, was in kindergarten, he came home one day and announced proudly to my daughter Terri that he had been named student of the week. Terri praised him effusively, and off he went, smiling. A few minutes later he was back. "Mommy," he asked, "what's a student?"

In the way of the very young, Mathieu had not been afraid to ask such a basic question. Whenever we're approaching something new, it serves us to reclaim an innocent curiosity. This allows us to be open to learning about even simple things. It makes us teachable.

Taking the first steps on your path from fiscal chaos to financial clarity and well-being can feel like a daunting task. The problem can seem insurmountable. Where to start? But with beginner's mind you'll be able to welcome the simple ideas and solid steps that make the journey possible.

Fortunately, the first steps of this process require nothing more than self-reflection. I ask each new client to do the following three things:

1. Identify your situation.
2. Define what you'd like to accomplish.
3. Get started by becoming conscious of and connected to your money.

Doing these tasks thoughtfully and thoroughly sets a strong foundation for the work ahead. For now, we'll focus on the first two, and we'll tackle the third in chapter 4.

Identify Your Situation

When I meet new clients, I listen as they share their stories and describe how much of their lives they spend worrying about money and how they feel like a failure for not being able to manage this problem. I hear about the terrible impact their relationship with money is having on their health, their family, and their emotional well-being. They often tell me they're ready to change things — that they just can't take it anymore.

I'm often impressed with how bright, accomplished, and talented my clients are — a continual reminder that a troubled financial relationship is almost never a problem of not being *smart* enough.

At this point we may talk about the consequences they are about to suffer because of their financial chaos. Perhaps they feel crushed by debt, can't seem to save money, or just don't know where their money goes. Creditors might be calling. An attorney or accountant may have told them that bankruptcy is their only remaining option. They may have already depleted their home equity loan or inheritance. Foreclosure on their house or business may be looming. They may have watched their assets dwindle because of overspending or because they want to meet their long-cherished goal of owning a home, traveling, or retiring with security. They know they've made mistakes with their money; that's why they've sought financial counseling.

I'll say to you what I've said to clients — and it's always proved to be true. At the start, neither of us knows the exact solution to your money problems. But as you work through the steps in this book, solutions that you can't imagine right now will become apparent. You can't yet see the entire path, but I absolutely know what the first steps are — and they work. So, let's take it one step at a time, starting with the following exercise.

EXERCISE

What's Not Working?

In your money journal, write the following questions and then take as much time as necessary to thoroughly answer them.

1. WHAT'S NOT WORKING IN MY RELATIONSHIP WITH MONEY?

As you consider this question, you might want to ask yourself things like: Am I always worried? Coming up short all the time? Do I feel financially insecure? Do I feel out of control with my spending? Is my debt burden what's troubling me? Or do I just crave a feeling of well-being and calm in my financial life?

2. WHAT EMOTIONAL AND PSYCHOLOGICAL CONSEQUENCES AM I EXPERIENCING?

Ask yourself these specifics: Am I unable to sleep because I'm worried about money? Am I having conflicts with my loved ones? Stress-related health problems? Are money troubles stopping me from being happy and enjoying life? These factors are hard to quantify but must be factored into your current money picture. The gains of engaging in this process are not just financial.

3. WHICH OF THE SYMPTOMS OF FINANCIAL DIS-EASE HAVE I EXHIBITED?

Consider: Have I been ignoring the reality of my financial circumstances, pretending that they will somehow, magically, get better? Have I felt obsessed with my money problems? Have I lost control of my spending, finding myself making purchases I can't afford, even though I've promised myself I wouldn't do so? Have I suffered painful consequences of my financial behavior but still fallen back into the same behavior?

Define What You Want to Accomplish

After people have told me the trouble they're experiencing, I ask them to imagine themselves in the future. I ask them, "When you look back, and you realize that Financial Recovery has been the best investment of your time, energy, and money (T.E.M.), what will you have accomplished? How will you know this has been a success?" So I invite you to visualize yourself in the future. Imagine you've applied the principles of Financial Recovery to your relationship with money. How will you know that this has been a worthwhile investment of your T.E.M.? What does success look like for you?

Getting these thoughts down on paper gives you something concrete by which you can later measure the success of your Financial Recovery process. The next exercise is designed to help you do this.

EXERCISE

What Would Success Look Like for You?

Write "Signs of My Ideal Financial Recovery" at the top of a page in your money journal. Then write this: "I will know that Financial Recovery has been the best investment of my time, energy, and money because..." Here you will list those experiences, practices, and accomplishments that will tell you that your process has been successful. Take the following questions into account.

- How will you behave around money?
- What will be the measurable differences in your life?
- How will you feel about your relationship with money?
- How will you spend your time?

Be as specific as possible. This list is completely personal, reflecting your own needs and desires for how you want to live.

When I ask clients to do this during our first meeting, some people start by listing "things" they want — a new car, a house, or some other purchase. But with a little prodding, nearly everyone starts to shift their ideas about what successful Financial Recovery would look like. They say things like, "I'll be able to manage my bills," or, "I'll no longer have debt," or, "I'll be current with the IRS," or even, "I won't be worried about money all the time."

Maybe you crave something seemingly simple, such as getting a good night's sleep without worrying about money. You may imagine living without the burden of family fights about money. Perhaps you long for the feeling of security and the financial freedom to make choices you desire. Is it that you want to get out of debt, or that you want to have savings? Or would you just like to know where your money goes and feel more in control of it? Do you want to be a role model for your kids so that they don't struggle with money in the future? A healthier relationship with money might allow you to leave a soul-crushing job or live where you choose. Do you dream of buying a home? Traveling? Starting a business? Funding your retirement? Contributing to a cause that has meaning for you? No dream is too big. No detail is too small.

Keep your journal handy so you can refer to this list later. You'll use it along the way to remind yourself of your goals and to recognize your progress.

Allowing Creative Solutions to Unfold

I'll let you in on a little secret: when you put the principles of Financial Recovery into practice, your dreams can become actual possibilities, even realities. You may also find that new aspirations and opportunities emerge — goals you may not yet be able to imagine. What is truly and deeply important to you will reveal itself along your course. And some of it might surprise you. Lila found an unexpected solution to her debilitating debt.

CASE STUDY

Lila

Lila was very discouraged at our first meeting. As a high school English teacher, she was convinced she'd never be able to pay down a debt that was more than twice what she earned in a year. Lila lived with her longtime partner, Sheila, in a small house that Lila owned. "I'll be paying off this debt for the rest of my life," she said. "And there's no way I can tell Sheila about it. If she knew I was in this much debt, she might leave me."

I said to Lila what I always say. "Neither of us knows all the answers yet. Outcomes and solutions that neither of us can imagine will begin to unfold as we work together. Trust the process. And let's just take it step by step." Lila agreed.

Lila started by assessing her current situation. We got the snapshot of her account balances, including her debt, along with how much she earned. From there, she began working through the steps of the process, and before long she felt the need to tell Sheila the truth about her financial situation. "I realized I was hiding it from her, and that's not the kind of relationship I want." This wasn't surprising. Lots of people feel less comfortable with keeping their money secrets as they go through the Financial Recovery process.

"You'll never guess what happened," Lila said. "Turns out Sheila's always felt weird just living in my house — like it was mine and not ours. She wanted to feel that we were sharing the investment in our home and our future. When I told Sheila about the debt, she asked if she could buy in on the house so we'd own it together. I used her contribution to pay off my debt. We now co-own the house, and I don't have any debt. I never would have thought of this solution. Now Sheila and I are both working on Financial Recovery together."

Neither Lila nor I imagined that part of the solution to her financial issues was living under her own roof. It's important to note that until Lila got an accurate assessment of her true financial picture (one she'd been hiding from for a very long time) and embraced a plan of being truthful and realistic about her money, Sheila's financial contribution would not have had the same impact. If Sheila had just paid down the debt, for example, and Lila had resumed her former spending behaviors, she might have landed in the exact same soup a few years down the line. And the consequences to their finances and their relationship could have been disastrous. Instead, both aspects of their lives were strengthened.

Commitment to a course of action combined with faith will bear unanticipated fruit. You've taken the first steps on the road to Financial Recovery. Imagine the creative resolutions that await you!

CHAPTER TWO

Déjà Vu All Over Again

Does Your Relationship with Money
Plunge You into the Money/Life Drain?

If you always do what you've always done,
you'll always get what you've always gotten.

— **COMMON RECOVERY SAYING**

When patterns are broken, new worlds emerge.

— **TULI KUPFERBERG**

Countless people live within an unsustainable, unstable financial structure. These unstable structures are characterized by feelings of anxiety and worry. They are signs of a predictable and progressive downward spiral in which the same money problems keep recurring despite attempts to change them.

Those caught in this downward spiral commonly feel that the demands on their time, energy, and money leave nothing that makes life worth living. Because they are unable to save and feel pressured to work more and earn more, their relationships become strained, stress compromises their health, and ultimately their overall quality of life deteriorates. They often feel hopeless and overwhelmed. I see this pattern all the time in people from all walks of life, in all lines of work, even people of wealth.

The late Michael Jackson was arguably one of the most iconic entertainers of our time. His music and talents generated a personal fortune that, by anyone's standards, should have been enough. But in the months after his death, it was widely reported that Jackson was millions of dollars in debt. His famous Neverland Ranch was headed for foreclosure. The state of his health was highly questionable, his weight so low that he often wore multiple layers of clothing to hide it, and he was reportedly dependent on a variety of pharmaceutical drugs. The last months of his life were spent preparing for a worldwide tour. I can't help but wonder how much pressure he felt to generate more money and how much this pressure (in addition to his drug use) contributed to his lack of sleep and deteriorating health. He had not released a new album in many years. He had creditors hounding him and was responsible for supporting not only his children but also an entire business empire with many employees. Despite his poor health, he must have felt tremendous pressure to work more and earn more.

If you're struggling with money, you may think you have little in common with Michael Jackson or other celebrities and professional athletes who end up in financial trouble. However, I have found that many of the same issues are present for anyone struggling with money issues. The numbers may be higher for the rich and famous, but the emotional toll is the same for everybody. The purchases may be grander, but the drive to spend beyond our means is the same. The lifestyle might be more extravagant, but the loneliness, shame, and sense of isolation can be experienced by anyone, no matter the quantity of money in his or her bank account.

In the months leading up to the culmination of my own financial crisis, I felt the overwhelming pressure of the life I was leading. I couldn't sleep because my mind was so cluttered with obsessive thoughts about how I could juggle money just to make ends meet. Despite the growing pressure, I continued to spend money in ways that made no logical sense given my circumstances.

People whose relationship with money is compromised or problematic often feel enormous pressure to make more money or to spend less. They experience a sense of increasing pressure and escalating emotions, especially worry and anxiety. Often clients describe the feeling of being caught in a downward spiral. I have come to call this the Money/Life Drain.

What It Means to Be Caught in the Money/Life Drain

Certain beaches have warnings posted that advise swimmers of the risk of being pulled underwater by a powerful force. What appears on the water's surface as an inviting opportunity to enjoy a swim can actually pose a dangerous, even deadly, hazard down below. That's how the Money/Life Drain begins. At first, spending a bit too much or accumulating a little debt can seem fine. But then the momentum begins and we find that we are swirling downward. Sometimes we're pulled downward because of circumstances beyond our control, such as a loss of income or a downturn in the economy. At other times the force is created by our own habits of spending or debting. However it starts, the force of the Money/Life Drain can grow powerful and we can feel defenseless against it.

The Money/Life Drain is depicted in figure 2.1. A triangle set precariously on its point, it represents an unsupported — and unsupportable — financial structure born of unhealthy money behaviors and circumstances. The force of the Money/Life Drain, with increasing pressure and narrowing options, draws us down to its bottom level. At this bottom, we feel trapped, caught in a repeated pattern of money behaviors and the consequences that come with them.

Let's look at the layers of the Money/Life Drain, starting at the top.

FIGURE 2.1. THE MONEY/LIFE DRAIN

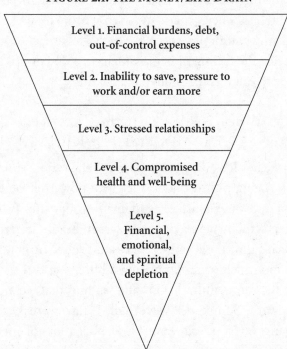

LEVEL 1. FINANCIAL BURDENS, DEBT, OUT-OF-CONTROL EXPENSES: We start our descent into the Money/Life Drain with feelings of being burdened. Our expenses are growing and we are having trouble keeping up. We might be juggling funds, using credit cards or family loans just to stay afloat. These provide momentary relief, but then the problems resume. Worry about money becomes a distraction. But despite our sincere intentions, our money habits don't seem to change. Bills continue to mount and creditors expect to be paid.

LEVEL 2. INABILITY TO SAVE, PRESSURE TO WORK AND/OR EARN MORE: The pressure increases and the options narrow. We can't seem to save money. It's hard to keep up with, much less get ahead of, our financial difficulties. Obtaining money by borrowing against the equity on our homes or by tapping retirement accounts, once unthinkable, now seems necessary. We feel pressure to get more money by working more hours or getting a second job. Even if we do this, the pressure doesn't subside. Working longer may also mean that we have to pay more child-care costs, commute costs, or other expenses that result from having less time to manage things. We're exhausted, but still the problems continue to grow.

LEVEL 3. STRESSED RELATIONSHIPS: We argue more — and more heatedly — with our loved ones. If we're trying to hide how bad our finances really are, the burden of the secret wears on us and we live in fear of being discovered. Friends or family members might grow impatient with our repeated inability to "get our act together." We have little time for people we love, which adds to a sense of isolation.

LEVEL 4. COMPROMISED HEALTH AND WELL-BEING: Worry about money is now starting to affect our sleep and our mood. Insomnia and anxiety add to our exhaustion. We suffer headaches or digestive troubles, elevated blood pressure, chest pain — or even panic attacks. We might turn to alcohol, drugs, or other distractions to escape the feelings of dread that seem nearly constant.

LEVEL 5. FINANCIAL, EMOTIONAL, AND SPIRITUAL DEPLETION: Finally, we are overwhelmed on every level. We experience down-to-the-bone exhaustion and feel depleted financially, emotionally, and spiritually.

The Money/Life Drain illustrates that an unhealthy pattern of relating with money can affect every aspect of our lives. This is true wherever we may be on the economic spectrum. It's true of a single parent struggling to live on a limited income. It's equally true for those who have tremendous financial resources but are not managing them.

Some caught in the Money/Life Drain are in a constant cycle of debt. It feels as though they can never pull themselves out of the drain. Others may have no debt at all but feel that they are not in control of their spending or that their life's purpose has been undermined by financial patterns that don't sustain them. Some feel that they're watching their resources disappear before their eyes. Some may be on the brink of financial disaster, while others may simply feel a nagging sense that their relationship with money is causing unnecessary anguish or keeping them from fully enjoying the benefits of a secure financial life. The Money/Life Drain looks different for different people, but the feeling can be the same.

Melanie is an example of someone caught in the early levels of the Money/Life Drain.

CASE STUDY
Melanie

Melanie had a thriving real estate business with a stupendous sales track record. Despite the fact that she was a star in her agency, she couldn't seem to get ahead. Between commissions, she and her family lived on credit cards, keeping no track of what they spent. When she made a sale, Melanie's sizable commission would pay off her debt. She'd bring every balance back to zero. This yo-yo debting went on for years. As her commissions grew, so did the size of the debt. She thought she was doing the responsible, sensible thing by paying the cards off each time, but as the pattern went on, she realized that even large commissions barely covered the debt accrued between sales, leaving nothing for ongoing living expenses, let alone savings. The charge cards had become her standard form of payment. Eventually, it was hard to feel excited about a big sale because the money was already spent. Melanie was caught in a repeating pattern. No matter how hard she worked, how many sales she made, she could never get ahead and feel safe, secure, or successful. That's the experience of being caught in the Money/Life Drain.

As Melanie's situation shows, the Money/Life Drain is not always about catastrophic financial circumstances; Melanie and her family were not in financial crisis, but they eventually could have been if she had not changed her unhealthy pattern of money behaviors.

THE THREE CONDITIONS THAT PULL US DOWN THE MONEY/LIFE DRAIN

How do so many of us find ourselves in the vortex of the Money/Life Drain? I've observed three basic categories of behaviors that land us there:

- Underearning
- Overspending
- Chronic Debting

The following sections examine each of these tendencies in detail.

Underearning

When some people hear the term *underearning*, they get an image of someone chronically unemployed, lolling on a sagging couch, eating from a giant bag of chips and watching TV all day. But this is not what I'm talking about here. Underearners are sometimes among the hardest working of my clients. Many have multiple jobs or work long hours with little time for themselves. In addition to working, they may serve as volunteers for philanthropic organizations or community projects. Some are self-employed professionals — therapists, physicians, even accountants or financial advisers — with educations and licenses that could and should be helping them to have profitable practices with stable, secure incomes. Others hold traditional jobs with regular paychecks.

Thomas was an underearner and a longtime client of mine.

CASE STUDY

Thomas

Thomas was spending about seventy thousand dollars a year on living expenses while actually netting only twenty thousand as an attorney. He was a respected lawyer of significant enough caliber that he had argued — and won — a case in front of the California Supreme Court. Even with his incredible accomplishments, Thomas was often so moved by the stories of those who sought his services that he had difficulty charging his full fees. He wanted to help them.

Thomas had received an early inheritance but had given a large portion of it away. When he first arrived for financial counseling, he had no idea how much he was spending or earning because he relied on his inheritance to cover the shortfall, thereby masking the consequences of his financial choices. When I asked him about his decision to give away some of his inheritance, Thomas cited the political affiliations of his youth and the fact that some of his peers, who were heirs and activists, were also giving their money away. Thomas noted that he felt ambivalent about his inheritance. "I felt guilty, I suppose, at having a lot of money when other people didn't, and I wanted to put the money to good use." Thomas also mentioned that he had a "complex" relationship with his father, whom he said was driven by capitalism. "I felt that the way our money had been acquired wasn't quite ethical. My father would basically buy a lot of land and then clear-cut the timber for sale. It could have been done on a sustained-yield basis so that it didn't harm the environment."

Despite his professional success, Thomas seldom took vacations, often taking off less than one week a year. He drove a seventeen-year-old car spattered with dings. His home was in disarray and cluttered, and he had no curtains. It seemed difficult for Thomas to allow himself to have or enjoy anything that money — even his own hard-earned money — could buy.

Despite working in a high-paying profession, Thomas was an underearner caught in the Money/Life Drain. He needed to find a way to keep true to his value of helping others while still honoring his own financial needs.

Underearners compromise their financial circumstances by accepting less for their work than it is worth, and often less than they need to live the way they want and deserve to. They commonly have difficulty setting limits, saying no, or asking for what they need and deserve, as was the case for Maggie.

CASE STUDY
Maggie

Maggie was a family therapist. She had a full practice and worked long evening and weekend hours to accommodate her clients' schedules. She worked hard but never seemed to make enough money to feel stable in her financial life. The bulk of Maggie's clients were at the lowest level of her sliding scale. On top of that, she had trouble following through with collecting fees. Many of her clients were substantially behind in their payments to her. Maggie felt responsible to her clients and sympathetic to their limited financial means. "It doesn't feel right to hassle clients because they can't pay their bills," she said. In addition to her practice, Maggie spent one full day a week and one weekend a month volunteering at a local shelter for battered women, providing free counseling services. As a result, she had overly full caseloads on her office days. Her weekends of volunteer work often left her feeling exhausted and wrung-out before her first client arrived on Monday.

Maggie was uncomfortable talking about money, so she didn't communicate clearly with her clients about payment arrangements. When they didn't pay their bills, it put Maggie in the awkward position of being both their therapist and their creditor. The problem worsened as she continued to see clients while their unpaid balances grew. She loved her work, but she felt ambivalent about charging for it. Though

Maggie was honorable in her intentions, her lack of financial clarity had become an issue in her work and in her relationships with clients. It's often hard for those in helping professions to see what they do as a business — even when their helping work is their career and livelihood.

Both Thomas and Maggie are classic underearners. But this condition isn't present only for those who are self-employed. My practice is full of clients who, though highly educated, work at unsatisfying, low-paying jobs. Others, hardworking and talented in the extreme, seem barely able to earn enough to scrape by. They undervalue their work, give it away, don't know how to advocate for themselves by negotiating appropriate salaries, and can't imagine asking for a raise or seeking a promotion.

Many underearners don't understand that healing their relationship with money is crucial to becoming financially successful. Translating personal and professional success into financial success is often the struggle for underearners. They may also have conscious or unconscious negative assumptions about people who seem financially successful.

In *Overcoming Underearning*, author Barbara Stanny writes of her surprise over the feelings that arose when her agent proposed a book idea about women who made a lot of money. "I immediately hated it. I pictured cold, aloof, designer-dressed snobs, leagues above me, totally intimidating if not downright boring. Then it hit me. If this is what I thought of successful women, how would I ever let myself become one? This was my first inkling that my own beliefs could be holding me back."[1]

In the course of my work with her, Maggie too unearthed some of her prejudices about those with money. Specifically, she discovered that she viewed those who had little money in a positive light. "People who don't have much have to work so hard, and other people just take advantage of them. It's not fair. They try to do the right thing and live honestly, but the system is set up to keep them down. It's only right to help them."

Maggie was operating from an assumption of what many have called "noble poverty." In fairy tales and popular movies — such as *Cinderella*, *Pretty Woman*, *101 Dalmations*, and even the Christmas classics *It's a Wonderful Life* and *A Christmas Carol* — the most wicked characters are the wealthy, particularly those who are born to wealth. On the other hand, the noblest characters are those who are poor. There is occasionally a virtuous wealthy person in these stories, but he is the exception. And by the end of the story he often sees the light and either rescues or assists the poorer, nobler hero or heroine or even relinquishes his fortune to join the simpler, more virtuous life.

The fascinating book *The Financial Wisdom of Ebenezer Scrooge*, by Ted Klontz, Rick Kahler, and Brad Klontz, examines our assumptions about wealth and poverty. The authors refer to these assumptions as "money scripts" and suggest that many of them (accurate or not) originate from classic tales that support the idea of noble poverty.[2]

Unconsciously buying into the idea of noble poverty, Maggie assumed that those with less are somehow more virtuous than those with more and that they are usually victims of the more affluent. I invited her to consider the implications of this assumption: "If you assume people with a lot of money are bad and people with little are noble, doesn't it make sense that you might behave in ways that keep you from becoming successful yourself?" As was the case for Maggie, the notion of noble poverty leads many to become underearners and eventually get caught in the Money/Life Drain.

Overspending

Overspending means spending more than you have, spending more than you intend to, or spending in ways that just don't feel right for you. Most overspenders spend more than they can afford, living beyond their means. They often spend more than they want to spend, perhaps to a degree that feels out of sync with their value systems. The buying patterns of many overspenders keep them from meeting financial goals that they've said are important. They often spend out of impulse or habit rather than in a way that feels within their control. Overspending can cause not only negative financial consequences but crippling emotional pain as well.

In many cases, although they're spending excessively, overspenders may not be doing so in a way that meets their real needs. They may be buying a lot of *pretties* but going without *necessaries*. This tendency is like putting up wallpaper in a house with faulty wiring. It looks nice, but deeper problems lurk beneath, which may cause an inferno. Some find that their money seems to disappear and they have nothing to show for it. Others splurge to feel that they're getting long-overdue rewards. Spending eventually feels as though it's gotten out of control. Shopping becomes a preoccupation.

Overspending leads to unmanageable debt or depleted assets, as it did for Josh.

CASE STUDY

Josh

Josh was busy studying for his professional engineering test — the final hurdle to obtaining his graduate degree. After graduating from Stanford University, he landed a new position as a project engineer, working under a partner in a prestigious San Francisco engineering firm. While his salary was still modest by Bay Area standards, it felt like a fortune to Josh after years of scrimping to get through school. The firm's partners thought highly of his work. Josh secretly harbored a goal of becoming the firm's youngest partner by age thirty-five, or maybe even having his own firm down the line. But first he had to pass his boards. As soon as he got his license, his salary would get a good bump — the first of many raises Josh foresaw in his promising future.

Josh decided he deserved a reward. After all, he worked hard all week and studied on weekends. On his way home, he took a detour through Union Square, San Francisco's prestigious shopping district, and found his way to Macy's. He'd soon be making presentations to potential business clients and wanted to look the part. Josh liked the way he felt leaving the store in his gray cashmere sweater and slacks — successful and stylish.

Over the months, he found that his commute home more regularly included a detour to Union Square. Each time he finished a project or got a bit of praise from a partner, Josh would say to himself, "I deserve a little reward." By now he had taken his boards and was just waiting for the results — and the raise that would soon follow.

A few weeks later, when Josh's charge card was declined, he shrugged it off as the credit card company's error. Humiliated, Josh asked the saleswoman to hold his selections, saying he'd be back after he straightened out the misunderstanding.

When he got home he opened his statements and took his first good look at the totals. He'd been making minimum payments, but in just a few months he had exceeded the limits on *three* cards. He added it all up and realized he owed more than five months' salary for the clothing and other items he'd charged. If he made even the minimum payments on the cards that month, he would not have enough for his rent and student loan payment. To make things worse, Josh discovered another envelope that had been hidden between the unopened credit card bills. It was from the state licensing board. He ripped it open. *"We regret to inform you…"*

On the surface, fixing overspending seems like a no-brainer, doesn't it? *Just don't spend so much. Do the math. Spend less than you earn and save the difference.* But this is like telling someone struggling with a weight problem to not eat so much, or someone who has a pattern of choosing abusive partners to date nicer guys. Aren't these the obvious, logical solutions?

In working with people over the past two decades I've observed that chronic overspending comes from a deep internal state of longing. The overspender keeps trying to fill an emotional void by buying things. At first, overspending can feel great. Buying lots of things creates the illusion of prosperity, abundance, and freedom. This illusion can cause people to feel as though everything is fine, and it can become highly addictive. As with chemical dependency, the first phase of overspending can often feel fun, exciting, and rapturously uplifting, but then the fun begins to fade. The overspender feels the pull of the Money/Life Drain.

Overspending can look very different for different people.

For Josh, it was buying clothes at Macy's. It could also be a grand-mother spending more than her fixed income by buying presents for her kids and grandchildren, or a sports fan buying too many collectible vintage baseball cards. Even those who have enough money to pay for their purchases can be overspending if their money behaviors create negative emotional or financial conse-quences. To make matters worse, modern technology has created a whole new style of overspending. That's what Lydia got caught in.

CASE STUDY
Lydia

Lydia's personal and work email inboxes were always filled with one-time deals and special offers. The bargains were amazing, and when she signed up for the various rewards programs she got free shipping. She received notices of pro-motions before they were announced to the general public. Lydia would get to work early to log on and see what selec-tions Amazon.com had recommended for her based on her most recent picks. Even big purchases required only a few keystrokes. She started skipping lunch with her colleagues, finding that she'd rather sit at her desk and browse. Search-ing for and ordering items gave Lydia a thrill, and she became adept at the hunt. She'd lose track of what she spent and the things she bought, so when packages arrived (an almost daily occurrence) it felt like Christmas. Lydia knew her FedEx and UPS drivers by name and even made the occasional thank-you purchase for them. It was fun to hand over a package just after signing for it and say, "This one is for you."

Eventually Lydia found that the arrival of packages be-came mundane. Often her parcels from Pottery Barn and

Crate and Barrel stacked up unopened in a spare bedroom. She even sometimes ordered the same items twice because she'd forgotten she'd already bought it. After a while, when the shipments arrived, Lydia no longer felt comforted by her purchases. She felt depressed, alone, and foolish. Her garage was full. Her house was cluttered with boxes. Though at this point Lydia had enough income to pay for her purchases, the impulsive quality of her spending felt unmanageable. She'd promised herself she'd stop making excessive purchases, but her promises were repeatedly broken when the next "special offer" arrived in her inbox. Internet shopping kept Lydia from using her money in ways that would meet her deeper needs. She wasn't saving money, and she hadn't been able to enjoy a vacation for a very long time.

Overspenders are often unable to admit to themselves that their purchases are ruining their lives. Buying things helps mask their painful feelings so they can avoid facing them, thus reducing their psychic pain. Many overspenders are unconscious of this motivation, and they try to overcome their spending habit but are unable to do so. It has become a way of life for them. Eventually, the added baggage of shame sets in.

Overspenders usually have a conflict between their exterior facade and their inner self. Whatever the obsession that has led them to overspend — clothes, cars, home decor, fine dining, jewelry, or other things — they typically feel they love their lifestyle but despise their life. They attempt to possess all the trappings that they believe *should* fill the emptiness they feel, and no matter how much overspenders earn, their lifestyles evolve to demand that they spend more. This often leads to chronic debting.

Chronic Debting

The popular 1958 horror movie *The Blob* portrays an alien life-form that resembles a blob of jelly, which at first doesn't seem very scary. But as the movie progresses and the blob grows to more and more astounding proportions, you begin to see its real menace. The blob takes over. It oozes its way into every nook of the town, into every home, church, and school. The constant pressure of the blob pushes locked doors open, breaks through dams, busts through unbreakable barriers, crushing and suffocating every living thing in its path. The blob is relentless.

Chronic debt is like the blob. At first it seems benign. But progressively, by its sheer mass and constant growth, it takes over our lives. It crowds out our financial stability and emotional well-being, affecting the quality of our lives.

Sonya's struggle with chronic debting drew her into the Money/Life Drain.

CASE STUDY
Sonya

Sonya's husband was often away on business. It made sense for her to handle the household finances, but she loathed the task. She often put off paying the bills until late notices arrived. Then she would pay the late fees and chide herself for accumulating extra expenses. When she paid bills, Sonya didn't bother to keep a running checkbook balance, figuring that the bank was better at calculations than she was. She'd just check the ATM to see what the balance was on a given day. It wasn't long before she lost track of her balance altogether and checks were cashed only because of her bank's overdraft protection. Each overdraft came with a penalty. One time, a check for only ten dollars to her daughter's school ended up costing fifty dollars in fees.

Late fees and interest seemed to eat the credit card payments Sonya made, and even though she paid more than the minimum amount, the balance never seemed to go down. When her credit card company called, Sonya felt embarrassed. She could imagine her husband's anger and disappointment at how she'd made such a mess of things. To appease the creditor, Sonya agreed to an instant withdrawal from her checking account that left her without enough money to cover the already-late power bill. But that would just have to wait. "They don't shut off the power right away," she reasoned to herself. To make it all worse, Sonya left work one day to find that her car had been booted because of unpaid parking tickets. She borrowed four hundred dollars from her mom to get the boot removed and pay the fines. Her checking account was empty, bills were still unpaid, and it would be two weeks before another paycheck.

Sonya found herself avoiding her bills completely. As they arrived, she shoved them into a desk drawer so she wouldn't have to look at them. In the evening, after she'd spoken with her husband from the road, she'd unplug the phone to avoid the creditors who kept calling. It was easier to pour a glass of wine and disappear into the pages of a good book than to think about her financial mess.

Like many, Sonya slipped into chronic debting passively: she simply let bills accumulate. She never got around to managing her money. In cases like hers, regular monthly bills become debt, and debt becomes chronic debt.

For chronic debtors, the past-due notices and calls from creditors become a constant, nagging force in their lives. But instead of rising to take action to rid themselves of debt, chronic debtors avoid it, deluding themselves into thinking things will somehow, magically, get better. Bills from one month spill unpaid into the next. Penalties and late fees accrue. Parking tickets and DVD rentals sit unattended, accumulating little fines that become bigger fines. Bigger fines become enormous. Many chronic debtors go years without paying taxes, thereby "passively" accruing debt to the IRS. The debt stacks up, and even looking at it becomes so upsetting that chronic debtors just don't look anymore. Unable to cope with the overwhelming worry about debt, they just withdraw and go numb. More debt accumulates. The blob grows even more enormous.

Many chronic debtors develop exquisite skills of negotiation. They weave a colorful tapestry of truths and untruths to explain themselves to indifferent creditors — stories of late paychecks, sick grandmothers, ailing pets, multitudes of elaborate explanations about why the payment has, once again, not been made. People trapped in a chronic debting cycle beg, bargain, and charm their creditors, making promises they cannot possibly keep, to adhere to a new payment schedule or simply to mail the check by a certain date. They know even as they make the promises that those promises will go unkept.

PLUGGING THE DRAIN

If you're caught swirling on the not-so-merry-go-round of the Money/Life Drain, the real question is, How do I get out of this? Later chapters in this book detail the strategies for helping you to plug the drain of life-sucking financial problems. Those strategies include discovering the difference between needs and wants, practicing a lifestyle of money mindfulness, and building sterling money behaviors for lifelong financial wellness.

But the first step to getting out of the Money/Life Drain is to stop the spinning. Stand still, reflect, and ask yourself some questions about your financial life.

EXERCISE

Are You Caught in the Money/Life Drain?

I invite you now to take another look — a personal look — at the Money/Life Drain on page 40. Reflect on each of the levels in descending order. Do you identify with the conditions at each level of the drain? Do you see any troubling, recurring patterns in your financial life? Ask yourself the following questions and write your answers in your money journal.

LEVEL 1

- Are you feeling burdened by your financial circumstances or debt? If so, how?
- What difficulties are you having managing monthly expenses?
- Does your spending ever feel out of control or uncomfortable for you? How do you experience that?

LEVEL 2

- Does saving money seem difficult or impossible?
- Are you feeling pressure to work more or earn more money?

LEVEL 3

- Do your friendships or relationships with family members or business associates feel stressed because of your money issues? If so, how?

- Do you find that you often argue about money or hide
  your financial circumstances to avoid arguments? How
  does this affect your relationships?
- If you fear disappointing others because of your money
  situation, how does this affect your life?

LEVEL 4

- Are you experiencing physical, emotional, or psychological health–related consequences because of your financial circumstances? What are they?
- Are you having trouble sleeping? Are you experiencing
  panic attacks or obsessive thoughts and worries about
  money? Write about this.
- Are you unable to take care of your health needs (for example, preventive healthcare, dental care, medications, or
  insurance)? Describe.
- Do you find that you consume more alcohol, overeat, or
  engage in other physically harmful habits to avoid your
  worries about money? How does this affect your life?

LEVEL 5

- Are you feeling exhausted, depleted, or defeated about
  your financial life?
- Have you compromised any of your social, moral, or
  spiritual values because of your financial circumstances?
  Describe.
- Do you feel financially, emotionally, or spiritually depleted? Explain.
- Do you recognize an ongoing pattern in your current
  financial situation? Are you caught in the Money/Life
  Drain? How might your money behaviors be adding to
  the drain's downward pull?

MOST WHO ARE CAUGHT IN THE MONEY/LIFE DRAIN got there in large part because of a long series of financial choices and habits — and they are completely unaware of many of them. So, in addition to feeling overwhelmed, people also feel ashamed and foolish for letting things go so far. This just adds to the strength of the drain's pull. The good news is that if our attitudes and behaviors are high on our list of contributing factors to the problem, then changing these things can have a dramatically positive impact on our financial lives.

Fortunately, you get to design your financial life, starting now. I've seen many people pull themselves out from the depths of the Money/Life Drain. Initially they didn't feel strong enough to pull themselves out of the undertow of their financial lives, but by starting with a single step and committing to Financial Recovery, they developed more strength than they'd thought possible.

CHAPTER THREE

Healing the Wounds of Shame and Deprivation

The Key to Understanding Your Needs, Wants, and Deepest Desires

Everyone needs beauty as well as bread, places to play in and pray in, where nature may heal and give strength to body and soul.

— JOHN MUIR

Instant gratification takes too long.

— CARRIE FISHER

The most painful money problems that many people face defy logic. I've worked with intelligent, gifted, even brilliant people who felt that they *should* be able to look logically at their circumstances and figure out a way to change their money behaviors. But when it comes to long-standing struggles with money, intellect is rarely adequate to solve the problem. Thinking doesn't solve it. Working harder doesn't solve it. Obsessing and calculating don't solve it. That's because the problem did not spring from a lack of intelligence, a shortage of hard work, or an inability to solve problems. The most persistent money problems have nothing to do with how smart we are and often little to do with how hard we work. Our most destructive money behaviors come from something much deeper.

When we peel back the layers of our money behaviors and look at the emotional drivers that got us into the Money/Life Drain, we almost invariably find a profound sense of deprivation. Very often this deprivation is fueled by an even deeper, and more darkly cloaked, sense of shame.

Deprivation is the invisible force in the lives of nearly everyone struggling with money. This can be true whether they grew up with very modest means or in great wealth, whether they make a six-figure salary or are unemployed. Shame and deprivation are regularly at play in an unhealthy relationship with money and the financial dis-ease it brings. As long as we don't recognize the haunting effects of shame and deprivation, logical solutions to our money problems have little hope of being effective. We can think harder, work harder, run numbers until we are dizzy, to no effect. We might even be able to white-knuckle our way out of some money jams for a time, but shame and deprivation have a way of undoing our efforts, and we find ourselves right back where we started, with the hole of deprivation larger and the shadow of shame even darker.

When I look back to the period when I was caught in my own version of the Money/Life Drain, I know that deprivation and shame drove my money behaviors. I became obsessed with *figuring* my way out of the mess, constantly calculating how to cover my expenses but simultaneously spending on things as an attempt to rid myself of the agonizing emptiness of deprivation. Deprivation was born of my unmet needs and grew to be an insatiable beast. Shame kept me in hiding, where the beast lives best. The more I spent, the deeper the financial hole in which I found myself grew. I later came to understand that the reason my spending wasn't quelling the deprivation was that I was profoundly confused about the difference between needs and wants.

In fact, this confusion fuels the poor financial decisions many make when deprivation is driving them.

As I describe them, needs and wants are neither synonymous nor interchangeable. Meeting our needs is a vital aspect of a healthy relationship with money. Spending money on wants is often how people get themselves into, and keep themselves stuck in, the Money/Life Drain. Therefore, it becomes really important to distinguish between needs and wants.

In this chapter, we will look at the deep and pervasive forces of deprivation and shame and how they express themselves in our relationships with money. Learning how to meet our most essential needs is the most vital step in disarming deprivation and eliminating its power in our lives. When we sort our needs from wants (and this is a much more subtle operation than you might at first think), we can address deprivation at its core. As we learn to meet our deepest needs, we can uncover our truest and most profound desires and create a life of our own design. This internal work is an essential part of the process of Financial Recovery.

DEPRIVATION AND SHAME DEFINED

Deprivation means living in a state of emptiness and longing, which we may not even be aware of but which nonetheless drives our choices. Deprivation is the wound that develops when our most essential needs — physical, emotional, social, or spiritual — are not met, particularly when these needs are not met for a long time and even more so when this happens to us early in life. Very often, to understand how the seeds of deprivation were sown, we need to look to our childhood experiences.

When I was small, my father served overseas in the military. My mother was an alcoholic and unable to care for me. I was shuffled among various family members and was even in foster care at times. When I was three, and my parents divorced, my mother returned to Wisconsin and left me with grandparents in California. I later lived with my father and my stepmother for a time.

My father was also an alcoholic. His new wife lived up to the stereotype of the wicked stepmother. She was hostile and neglectful. We lived in a housing project in Sacramento, California, and with severe limitations of both financial and emotional resources, neither of my parents was able to provide for even the most basic needs of a child. Kitchen cupboards were locked (literally), so food was unavailable. Clothing was shabby. A serious kidney disease that ultimately resulted in the removal of one kidney caused me to wet the bed nightly. Because the adults in the household were inattentive to my condition, bedding went unchanged. It seemed I was always cold and hungry. The environment was emotionally, intellectually, and physically stark and hostile. This experience, for me, was deprivation on every level.

When I was ten, my Aunt Fran and Uncle Binnie took me into their home. They had two young children of their own to care for but did everything they could to give me all I needed and more — love, nourishment, a sense of belonging, and security. I'll never forget the comforting evenings enjoying hot Ovaltine and cold cereal and my aunt reading another thrilling chapter of the Bobbsey Twins at bedtime. This was far different from the squalid surroundings of the Sacramento housing projects with locked cupboards and wet bedding. My aunt and uncle fought for and gained guardianship of me, and in more ways than one, they saved my life.

This Dickensian story is mine, but many other children grow up with their needs unmet and have similar stories. In my case, the deprivation was obvious, but it can also take on a much more deceptive face. Deprivation is wily and a master of disguise.

Deprivation at Any Income Level

Many years ago I was taking a walk with a friend whom I'd met in a recovery program for people with money problems. He pointed out a four-story Victorian house on an acre of land, with its own private beach. When my friend told me that this was the house he'd grown up in, I first felt disbelief, then anger. This house was my fantasy! How could anybody have grown up in a house like that and ended up in the same place that I had found myself? As that initial flash of anger and confusion passed, I listened to the real story of my friend's childhood experience. He told me about his alcoholic, absent father and his overcontrolling mother, his feelings of isolation and loneliness — the ache of his unmet needs. In that moment, I realized that behind the very different walls of his home and mine, we'd both experienced the impact of neglect, abuse, and parental indifference. Though our journeys appeared completely different, we'd arrived at the same destination.

When I hear a story about someone's background, whether it was similar to or quite different from mine, I can often sense that deprivation has become an element of that person's life, including his or her relationship with money. By identifying unmet needs and learning to meet them, we can begin to heal those early wounds and grow beyond them.

ABUSE, NEGLECT, SHAME, AND MONEY

While an internalized sense of deprivation is often born of childhood experiences, or traumatic losses that can occur at any time in life, its shackles can retain their hold on us even if our financial circumstances improve. Decades after such experiences, the vestiges of deprivation linger. The deprivation can eventually take the form of self-neglect, overindulgence, or even addictive behavior.

For many of us, deprivation and shame lead us to create an

external reality that reflects our inner sense of worthlessness. We create outside circumstances that match our inside experience of deprivation. Some do this by underearning, keeping themselves unable to adequately provide for themselves. Others attempt to camouflage their feelings of deprivation by overspending, filling their closets, their garages, or their homes with things that disguise what they feel inside. Still others neglect their own needs while overspending on the needs of others. None of this actually feeds the insatiable beast of deprivation but instead only fortifies it.

In 2010, we all witnessed the tragic oil spill in the Gulf of Mexico. The sickening images of seabirds, mammals, and fish with feathers and skin covered with oil filled our TV screens. We watched in horror as the tender marshland grasses became saturated with black-brown goo. While the gusher was eventually capped, the viscous remnants of the disaster remain, requiring years, perhaps generations, of cleanup. As with this oil disaster, the residue created by neglect and abuse leaves the stain of shame on our spirits and self-esteem. Its gluey remnants cause us to believe that we don't deserve more. This stain can cling to us throughout our lives if we don't find the proper solvents to remove it. Just like those seabirds, miserable and flightless, many of us are unaware of the source of our discomfort. We may feel ashamed that we can't seem to manage our money or make healthier choices, and we cope by buying things. The solvent of "new stuff" is wholly inadequate to cut through the grime of deprivation and shame, but we keep trying anyway.

Those who survive childhood abuse often internalize the shame they feel. It can later manifest as a troubled relationship with money, work, and self-esteem. John Bradshaw's 1988 book *Healing the Shame That Binds You* was a longtime *New York Times* bestseller, remains in print, and continues to sell in huge numbers.

Of course, part of the reason is Bradshaw's skillful writing and insights into his subject. The much sadder reason for the book's continued success is that shame affects so many. "Toxic shame is true agony," he writes. "It is a pain felt from the inside, in the core of our being."[1]

Mary Beth McClure is a friend and skilled therapist with extensive experience in working with survivors of childhood abuse and neglect. "Many of us find that early-childhood experiences of trauma, neglect, and abuse impact our relationship with money," Mary Beth explained during an interview I conducted with her. "Experiences of shame or deprivation influence the person's belief in themselves about being successful." She went on to describe how those who have suffered abuse often find it difficult to believe that they "deserve good" because they were treated so badly. This confirmed what I have observed for years in the lives of my clients and their relationships with money.

> Shame is like everything else; live with it for long enough and it becomes part of the furniture.
> — SALMAN RUSHDIE

Danielle Ray is a psychotherapist and a certified Financial Recovery counselor. Much of her therapy practice is focused on recovery from child abuse. When I interviewed her about the role of shame and how it can affect how we relate to money, Danielle explained: "Shame, in my mind, is a primary hallmark of sexual abuse. People who have been abused often try to compensate for shame with money. In their minds, money tells the world that they're okay. They are trying to compensate for something, but it is never enough — they can never make up for what happened. This creates an endless cycle of never enough."

Another toll of child abuse and neglect is that they squelch a sense of hope and optimism about the future. Often survivors of abuse bring the helplessness they felt as children into their adulthood. They have a hard time imagining a future that is any different from their internal experience. If someone feels deprived, ashamed, and hopeless, is it any wonder that she might not spend money in a way that is healthy for her present, much less her future? The mere idea of having a future, to say nothing of a full and abundant one, seems but a gossamer dream that many abuse survivors cannot imagine ever becoming reality.

> *Trust me on this one.*
> *If you have any abuse in your history, you probably have a hard time looking into the future and seeing any realistic happy ending.*
> — **MOLLY FISK**

Underearning, overspending, and chronic debting can often stem from deep-rooted shame. Those who experienced childhood neglect or abuse often have a difficult time valuing themselves, and hence they struggle to earn the money that would serve in their own self-care. After all, if we feel worthless, why would we feel we deserve to have our financial needs met? What better than a negative balance, in the form of debt, to reflect back to us our feeling that we are without value?

I now know that shame drove much of my behavior with money. Through healing my relationship with money I began to understand my most basic needs and that I deserved to have them met — that I deserved to make enough money to nourish and take care of myself.

I've been honored to witness many similar transformations in those recovering from their own shame and deprivation. This is a big part of what has made my relationship with my work deeply satisfying and rewarding. I find that when abuse, neglect, and shame issues surface in our financial lives, the process of Financial Recovery can be an important part of overall personal healing too. People learn to treat themselves with respect, honor their needs, and recognize that they are deserving of having those needs met in healthy and appropriate ways. Of course, no amount of financial well-being will erase the experience of child abuse. Some survivors require a lot of support to recover from their pasts, and most survivors benefit from therapy. But addressing the financial symptoms of abuse or neglect can be an important part of a larger healing process.

You Can Never Get Enough of What You Don't Need!

Unmet needs, whatever their source, expand over time, ultimately becoming or amplifying deprivation. The world becomes a source of aching disappointment where we must desperately seek whatever crumbs of comfort we can find. Desperate attempts to fill the hole of deprivation take many forms. Some people accumulate things, buying and buying in a frenzied way. But they find that no matter how much they buy, their feeling of deprivation still remains. The reason is painfully simple: *You can never get enough of what you don't need.*

If what you need is a sense of security, filling your closet with new clothes won't provide that. If you're in need of companionship, excessive gift buying won't improve the quality of your relationships. While purchases themselves often do not meet our core needs, using our resources of time, energy, and money in healthy ways can be part of how we do meet them — sometimes with money and, many times, in ways that cost nothing at all. When we identify the actual areas of deprivation that exist in our lives, we can begin to form a plan to alleviate them. As we move into identifying needs and

> *What does not satisfy when we find it, was not the thing that we were desiring.*
> — C. S. Lewis

differentiating them from wants, this will become clearer. The strategies for meeting needs and eliminating deprivation will unfold in the following chapters.

Know this: You can't wait until your financial picture is completely better before you start addressing deprivation and your unmet needs. Even if it's in small and simple ways, you must start doing this as part of the first steps of Financial Recovery.

THE THREE SIGNS OF DEPRIVATION

There are three signs, or patterns of behavior, that people develop as they struggle with deprivation in their lives. These are:

- Doing without
- Making do
- Overdoing

Exploring how, or if, you are operating in one of these three states in your relationship with money can help you to identify areas of unmet needs. This is key, and perhaps the first and one of the most important steps to changing your ongoing relationship with money. As you read through the explanation and examples below, I invite you to reflect on your own financial life.

Doing Without

Doing without means not having something really essential. When we began our work together, my client Marilyn was doing without some very basic needs being met.

CASE STUDY
Marilyn

Marilyn was in her eighties when her husband, Hugh, died. Marilyn and Hugh had never earned a lot of money, but they had lived frugally and always tucked away money for the future. But in his final years, Hugh's medical bills had been so high that much of that savings was gone. The bills continued to come months after Hugh's death.

It was getting harder to make her Social Security check stretch, and the co-payments on her own blood pressure medications were a challenge. Marilyn started cutting her pills in half. That way, her prescriptions would last twice as long.

Marilyn's is a clear case of someone doing without a basic need being met. Hers is a tragic and far too common story of those whose financial lives are challenged by healthcare costs, which could happen to any of us.

Doing without can show up in daily living as neglecting to take care of basic needs of safety, health, and comfort, such as dental care, car repairs, or insurance. Ironically, in some cases people do without basic things while spending on seemingly less important things, which only worsens their circumstances. They may appear to "have it all," while important needs are not being met and a deep sense of deprivation grows.

Making Do

People who are in a state of *making do* habitually patch things together, trying to use inadequate substitutions to satisfy real needs. This is different from choosing to live with something less than perfect (or even without something) until it's a wiser time to make the purchase. This is about a lifestyle of tolerating poor or inadequate substitutions for things that are needed for comfort, security, and fulfillment. Making do is like using duct tape and baling wire to fix a jet engine. It might work for a short time, but it's certainly not the best or safest option.

In the healthiest sense, making do can describe adapting, improvising, being resourceful — making the best of a bad situation. That sounds like a good thing, right? And it can be. Flexible people know how to go to Plan B when Plan A doesn't work out. But like many behaviors that are adaptive at one point in life, making do can become maladaptive and even damaging when it's overapplied.

Making do, as I'm speaking about it here, is about self-neglect. It's about making substitutions that range from woefully inadequate to dangerous — even deadly. Making do with inadequate or even dangerous substitutions is not a viable Plan B.

Sometimes people confuse being frugal with making do. Being frugal could be resoling a favorite pair of shoes rather than buying new ones. Making do is buying a pair of shoes in the wrong color and half a size too small simply because they're on sale and hoping that the salesman can stretch them enough to fit. Some make-dos can even be dangerous. I worked with a client who tried to economize when her car needed new tires. Rather than buying new ones, she made do with a set of used tires with just a bit more tread than her old ones. This substitution resulted in a dangerous blowout on the freeway just a week after she'd bought the tires.

Often making do becomes a way of life — a constant feeling that you must tolerate the shabby, broken, or unpleasant because that is what is due you. Again, old feelings of shame are often at play here. I've encountered clients who make do by wearing clothing that is too tight because they feel undeserving of nice things until they lose weight. Others tolerate stained and broken furnishings that make them feel too embarrassed to have guests come to their homes. Tolerating these states of deprivation affects the quality of our lives and the ability to feel good about ourselves.

Overdoing

Many of us know the feelings that come with *overdoing*. These are feelings of being overwhelmed, frantic, or panicky. We're running late, running over, or running on empty. Overdoers live in a constant state of being overcommitted and overextended in terms of time, energy, or money — or all three. People often give kudos to the overdoer: "What would we do without you? I can't believe how much you do for everybody."

But overdoing has a dark side. Overdoers are often so busy running around taking care of things and taking care of others that their own needs remain unmet. They may have schedules crammed full of working overtime, volunteer work, or scrambling around with the tasks of caring for others. They may not get enough sleep, exercise, or good nutrition because there never seems to be enough time for *these* things. As we've already discussed, having unmet needs leads to a sense of deprivation, and deprivation often causes us to spend in ways that aren't healthy.

When spending is overdoing, it takes on a frenzied, addictive quality, and despite highly damaging consequences, the spender seems unable to change his behavior. The purchasing has a "piling on" aspect; if one would do, five would be better. Those who overdo often experience a snowball effect in their spending, and it feels like a compulsion — they can't stop, even though they really want to. Carly's story exemplifies overdoing.

CASE STUDY

Carly

Carly and her husband, Todd, agreed that they wanted her to be a stay-at-home mom. It meant planning their expenses carefully, but both of them wanted this for their family. After their daughter was born, Carly decided to make photo albums so that her daughter would have what she'd always lacked. Her few childhood photos were tossed haphazardly into a box. It was all her single mother had been able to manage between her two jobs. As a child, Carly had longed to be part of a happy family with the vacation photos and family portraits that some of her friends had.

Next to her grocery store she found a scrapbooking store that sold beautiful albums, paper, and cute accessories. She took a how-to class at the store and walked out with a trunkload of supplies. Her first baby album drew much admiration, and she loved knowing that her little girl would have it forever. Next, Carly made a Father's Day album for Todd. It brought tears to her eyes to see all the photos of her baby girl with such a loving daddy. There were no such pictures in Carly's one box of childhood photographs.

Carly stopped in the scrapbooking store almost every time she bought groceries. Sometimes she'd spend just fifteen or twenty dollars — sometimes a lot more. When she paid for groceries with her debit card, Carly would ask for cash back so she could go to the scrapbooking store and Todd would not see the expenditure. She'd tuck her new purchases away before he got home. They began to argue about money. "We're just not making it," he said to her. "We're going in the hole every month. I just can't figure out where all our money goes. I hate to say it, but I don't think we can afford to live on just one income."

Carly's overdoing was about to cause her to do without

the very thing she wanted to portray in her photo albums — a loving, secure family and a mom who was home.

Carly's internalized feeling of deprivation from her early life fueled her overdoing. While there is nothing wrong with her wanting to create and collect happy family experiences, her history of deprivation drove her to go overboard to the point that she was in jeopardy of losing her ability to be the stay-at-home mom she wanted to be. She was also compromising her values of honesty and trust in her marriage by being deceptive about how she was spending money. This added to her feeling of shame, but she felt unable to change the pattern.

Through our work together Carly began to identify her pattern of overdoing. I asked her, "How would it feel to do an album for yourself?" The tears in Carly's eyes told me, and her, that this touched on the area of real deprivation for her. Later, Carly decided to dig out her old box of childhood photos. Using the supplies she already had on hand, she created an album for herself. In doing this, Carly was identifying and facing her own deprivation. After making her album, Carly found that her frenetic buying subsided. She could enjoy making albums of her family without the urgency she'd felt before. She found it far easier to moderate her purchases and preserve the family life that she really treasured.

Hollywood has portrayed overdoing in the romantic comedy *Confessions of a Shopaholic*. But overdoing is no joke. It brings pain, causes families to fall apart, and erodes emotional, spiritual, and financial well-being. For overdoers, the compulsion to buy overrides the power to make a reasonable choice or change behavior. Because they can never get enough of what they don't need, they keep buying stuff, but it doesn't touch their real needs at all. So they buy more clothes, more toys, more goodies, but the feeling of deprivation remains. For many overdoers, their purchases are a thin veneer, giving the impression to the outside observer that everything is fine. In reality, they may be anything but.

THESE THREE STATES — doing without, making do, and overdoing — are not necessarily discrete; one person can exhibit all three kinds of behavior, even simultaneously. The results of all three are often the same: that old Money/Life Drain just keeps tugging us downward, and we are left with feelings of deprivation. Doing without, making do, and overdoing can eventually become our undoing.

WHAT DO YOU REALLY NEED?

Let me tell you what I have said to so many clients over the years: You deserve to live a life of satisfaction and abundance in which your needs are met. Understanding and learning how to meet your needs is elemental to eliminating deprivation and the unhealthy influence it may be having in your life. Spending your time, energy, and money in ways that meet your deepest needs cools the fever of deprivation and lets you feel a sense of peace and comfort. As you learn to meet your needs, you become better equipped to make wise and thoughtful choices about those things you want. But when you remain unaware of your needs or neglect to meet them, you perpetuate the cycle of shame and deprivation and keep yourself stuck in unhealthy money patterns. Remember, you can never get enough of what you don't need.

However, *need* is a tricky word. Of course, at the most basic survival level, needs are obvious, and most humans need essentially the same things: enough to eat, clean water, shelter, and good health for ourselves and our loved ones. But virtually all of us fortunate enough to live in developed communities, in modern conditions, long for satisfactions and comforts beyond our most basic biological needs.

Noted psychologist Abraham Maslow developed the concept of the Hierarchy of Human Needs.[2] Maslow's simple but insightful premise was that our most basic physiological needs must be met before our higher needs can be realized. Someone who is without adequate nutrition, living in danger, or not sure if he can provide for his family would probably not be able to imagine spending money on piano lessons or books of poetry. Someone in an abusive relationship, filled with daily threats to her safety, might find it nearly impossible to concentrate on studying art history or planning a restorative vacation. Maslow arranged this need progression into a hierarchy, with the most basic at the bottom (see figure 3.1). I've always appreciated that Maslow considered even the items at the top of his pyramid as part of the Hierarchy of Human Needs and not the hierarchy of *wants*.

I view the journey up Maslow's pyramid not as a linear progression in which we arrive at one level, stay there for a while, and then move on to the next, but rather as a process of ongoing growth and shifting levels. That is, in some areas of our lives we may be operating at very high levels, while in other areas we may be struggling on lower planes. Think, for example, of someone who is succeeding professionally, getting great acclaim and recognition. She feels competent and proud of her work and is gaining great rewards. But she is also a mother of a toddler, and her little one is teething. A full night of sleep is a fantasy. She and her husband have been arguing because they're both exhausted and irritable. There is little time to eat well or exercise, and she's

feeling frumpy and unattractive. As you can see, she is functioning at different levels of need in various areas of her life. At work,
she is enjoying acclaim and rewards, which boost her self-esteem.
She is intellectually challenged and stretched. But at home, at this
time in her life, she is feeling that her most basic physiological
needs are unmet.

FIGURE 3.1. MASLOW'S HIERARCHY OF HUMAN NEEDS

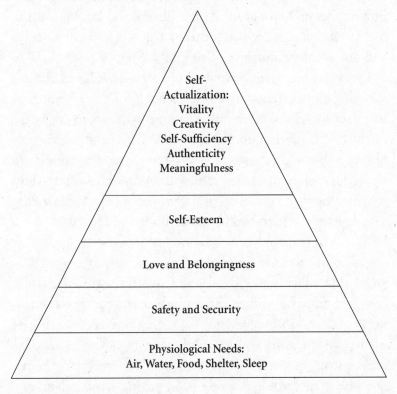

Also, needs are not one-size-fits-all. When we start to move
up the pyramid, what we require to meet our needs varies widely.
For one person, safety and security needs are met with a simple
home and basic furnishings. For another person, a home alarm
system and an electronic gate are important to feeling secure.

One person may feel that dressing fashionably is an important reflection of her self-esteem, while another feels that fashion is completely unimportant and is perfectly happy with thrift-store purchases. Perhaps massages or taking an annual meditation retreat may feel really important to one person's sense of spirituality. Another may value going to ball games with his family, so having season tickets may feel important for sharing experiences with his kids. Of course, those suffering in poverty or functioning without their most basic survival needs being met would see *all* these things as luxuries — wants, not needs.

Taking care of needs is not a simple checklist: Food, *check*. Safety, *check*. Self-esteem, *check*. Rather, understanding the difference between needs and wants will let you know and understand your evolving physical, emotional, intellectual, social, spiritual, and creative needs, and how to meet them. Getting in touch with your subtler needs is a natural part of the progression of Financial Recovery and follows logically behind understanding and meeting your more basic needs.

UNDERSTANDING THE DIFFERENCE
BETWEEN NEEDS AND WANTS

Many of us don't have a real understanding of the difference between needs and wants. And some people, especially those who feel shame about their history with money, feel undeserving of having either. In working with hundreds of clients struggling in their relationships with money, I've consistently found that the core of their problems is an inability to understand their own needs. When I ask clients about whether something they're spending money on (sometimes a great deal of money) is a want or a need, they respond with a blank stare, followed by the nearly universal question, "What's the difference?" After giving it a bit of thought, some people want to label everything but the barest of survival necessities as wants, while others feel that they absolutely need everything!

Spending on a myriad of things we want while leaving needs unmet is like grazing all day on snacks but never feeling fed. The constant snacking may exceed a recommended caloric intake, but we don't feel satisfied. By not understanding our nutritional needs, or even allowing ourselves to feel a sense of authentic hunger, we fail to nourish ourselves with a satisfying, nutritious meal. So too we might spend — or overspend — on a thousand things and still feel a hunger for a need yet unmet.

I've come to feel that a need is best defined by the person who feels it. But learning to ask ourselves and actually discern what our needs are is anything but black-and-white. It's subtle, nuanced, and highly individualistic. Sorting wants from needs and beginning to make decisions about them is more of an ongoing conversation with yourself than a checklist. It's a deep inner dialogue through which you come to understand yourself, your deepest longings, and your impulses. It involves reflection.

Like most people, at this stage, you may struggle with the distinction between your wants and your needs. That's okay. You can start wherever you are. We'll continue to hone this process through each of the phases of Financial Recovery.

To begin to sort out these tangled ideas, it helps to think of needs and wants this way:

- A need, when filled, *sustains* us.
- A want, when filled, *entertains* us.
- Attempting to substitute wants for needs eventually *drains* us.

Sometimes we come to know what a real need is only when we meet it or when we stop distracting ourselves by buying impulsively or out of blind habit. Spending money on wants alone is often the source of debt, bankruptcy, and a financial hole so deep that it swallows our lives. People become imprisoned by their wants, and in that prison they cannot make decisions about the true value or worth of an item.

The following guidelines and strategies may help you to sort your needs from your wants.

Our Deepest Needs Cannot Be Met by Spending Money

The need for laughter, companionship, physical touch, intimate confidants, spiritual connectedness, and other valuable but intangible treasures cannot be satisfied with purchased items. Loneliness, the need to feel close to someone, or the need for loving affection can drive spending that may otherwise defy logic. To feel loved, we may purchase extravagant gifts. To feel successful, we may buy a luxurious home. Buying things may make us briefly forget that we are lacking companionship. The encounters with friendly salesclerks, manicurists, or others who are involved in our financial exchanges may serve as imitations for the intimate relationships we are missing, providing the tiniest taste of the deep human connection we deeply long for. For a short time, these substitutions may work, but then the sense of deprivation creeps back up to the surface. So we keep buying.

> *Your friend is your needs answered.*
> — **KAHLIL GIBRAN**

Gotta Have It NOW? Then It's Probably a Want

When I think of wants, I think of immediate gratification. We see this in our kids, who see a commercial or a toy a friend has — something they've never seen or imagined before — and immediately *want* that item. Little ones can throw tantrums when they want something. Older kids can beg and plead, sometimes

wearing down their parents until they get the object they're obsessed with. As evidence that this particular item is a want, and
not a real need, the new toy or item is played with for a short
while but then rests discarded and forgotten, replaced by a new
craving for a new object.

Wanting things and craving immediate gratification are not
reserved for children. Adults too can see something they like and
then get overcome with wanting it. They don't know they want
the thing until they see it, but then they get the overwhelming
feeling of *want it, need it, gotta have it, NOW!* The urge to buy on
impulse is a good indication that something is a want, not a need.

By slowing down, looking inward, and discerning if that item
is a need or a want, you'll be able to vastly reduce the impulse
buys that often contribute to money struggles. This can be a
tough pattern to change, but the rewards for learning to delay
gratification are enormous. Being thoughtful about your purchases might mean that you delay getting more optional needs
met right away, but it can also mean that you ultimately get what
you *really* need.

Pleasures and Comforts Can Be Needs

Many of my clients, at first anyway, assume that Financial Recovery means that they no longer get to enjoy anything fun — especially while they're paying down debt. They have this idea that
I'm going to give them a list of what they are "allowed" to buy
— that I'm going to act as the unyielding guard in their Financial
Recovery prison.

No wonder people put off addressing their finances. Remember in chapter 2 how I talked about overspenders buying lots of
pretties instead of necessaries — the wallpaper instead of the wiring? The necessaries are important for taking care of our needs,
but who wants to go through life with absolutely no pretties? If

giving up all the fun, pleasurable things forever was required to heal your relationship with money, who would want to do this? This kind of strict, narrow thinking is what made it impossible for me to stick to the restrictive plan I first received from a credit counselor who put me on a budget as an attempt to fix my money troubles. It felt like a rigid money diet to which I couldn't stick because the plan was designed for my creditor's needs alone and not mine.

In reality, honoring needs doesn't necessarily mean forgoing pleasures and comforts. My friend Angela recently figured this out while looking for a new apartment. Her first impulse was to spend the bare minimum on rent. At first, she said that all she needed for an apartment was a "box on a bus line." But as she looked at apartments in the price range she originally set, Angela could see that they would be unacceptable. Yes, these apartments would meet her need of *shelter*, but her real need was to have a *home* where she would feel safe and comfortable and be proud to bring friends. Without these needs met, Angela would feel as though she were living in deprivation — not to mention that she would end up spending more money on eating out, since she wouldn't feel comfortable having friends over. So she took another look at her money situation, taking her real needs into account. She adjusted her original rent price range by 15 percent and was then able to find the perfect apartment — one that she could afford but that also met her need for a place that felt like home. Again, needs are not just about survival — they're also about being in touch with what is really important to you.

The "Do I Really Need This?" Challenge

When facing a decision about making a purchase, and to see if an item is a genuine need and not an impulsive want, ask yourself the following questions:

1. Do I really *need* this? In other words, is this a need or an impulse want? If I waited a week, a month, a year, would I still really *need* this?

2. Do I *really* need this? Note the new emphasis. This is asking about the degree of the need. Do I *really* need this enough that I should make it a priority? Do I *really* need this so deeply that I'm willing to give up something else in order to have it?

3. Do I really need *this*? The emphasis on the word *this* is to discern if the purchase of this particular item is an attempt to meet a need that is impossible to meet with material things. Am I feeling lonely, angry, anxious, rejected, or ashamed? Am I trying to mask a deeper feeling with a superficial purchase? If so, how could I take care of this need in a way that will actually bring me the comfort or emotional relief I long for?

If your answer to these three questions is, "Yes, I *do* need this," there is one more question to ask yourself:

4. Would buying this item be worth what I'd have to give up in order to get it? Asking yourself this question will keep you in touch with the finite nature of your money and the consequences of making selections. Each time you make a purchase, it affects your ability to have the other things, and sometimes to meet a more pressing or time-sensitive need. Once again, it's not that you can't have this new thing. It's just that if you choose to buy it, you're choosing to either forgo or delay spending on something else. It's up to you.

Awareness and deep understanding of your own needs and wants (and the ability to discern the difference) are like the soil needed to grow a healthy garden. Only when the soil is rich, cleared of weeds and rocks, can the tender seeds be planted and expected to grow.

Identifying and taking care of your needs is a skill that you will use for the rest of your life. Once you learn to meet your needs, you'll think differently about your wants and you'll be able to recognize them as the smoke screens they really are.

Understanding Your Needs Is an Inside Job

By distinguishing wants from needs and making sure that needs are met, you will find that you can climb up Maslow's Hierarchy, creating not only a life that meets your needs but one that is fulfilling on every level. The next, deceptively simple exercise will help you to do just that. If you do it thoughtfully and with deep reflection, it can give you great insight into what's important to you.

It's very common to hear the voice of our "inner critic" when we start thinking about or stating needs and sorting them from wants. You may have received early messages from either your cultural background or people in your life who made you feel bad about what you felt you needed. You may have felt judged or criticized for stating things that were important to you because your needs were different from those of others in your family or social circle. Perhaps you were made to feel that your needs were shallow, unimportant, or too big. What you need is highly individual. For now, I'll ask you to still the voices of those inner critics and allow yourself to play a little in this exercise.

EXERCISE

Creating a Needs and Wants List

I'd like to ask you to use your journal to create what I call a "Needs and Wants List." Divide a page of your money journal into two columns. Label the left column *Needs* and the right column *Wants*. (Or go to my website, www.financialrecovery.com, to download this page.)

Think about your current conditions: your home, transportation, clothing, health practices, relationships, spiritual life. Let yourself envision items or experiences that seem to be missing from your life. These can be small things like new walking shoes or bigger experiences like sharing a trip to Hawaii with a friend or loved one.

As an item comes into your mind, place it in one of the columns on your page. Don't worry about making a perfect list. You can always move items later. In fact, reflecting and revising your list is important and you'll find that the more you reflect, the more refined, clear, and specific your list will become. Having this clarity will inform every step you make on your journey of Financial Recovery.

If you're feeling especially stuck about a particular item and you don't know which category to place it in, enter it onto both lists and put an asterisk beside the entry. As you go on to the next chapters of this book, you'll continue to gain clarity and insight into this valuable process of sorting your needs and wants. The category those asterisked items belong in will become clear to you. What's important at this phase is to resist getting stuck. Just keep going and remember, this is *your* list.

CREATING A NEEDS AND WANTS LIST is not just an exercise. As you hone it, the list will become a valuable tool that will help you to make fully conscious, healthy choices about your spending. It will remind you of what is most important to you when you risk being swept into the frenzy of spending and consuming. Years into Financial Recovery, people continue to find keeping this list invaluable for maintaining a healthy relationship with money. This list will be useful in chapter 5 when you begin devising your individual plan for meeting your needs.

You can train yourself to ask, "Where is this on my Needs

and Wants List?" whenever you encounter a spending dilemma. When we don't have a list, our needs can sometimes feel like an enormous, undefined mass. We can be haunted with the horrible feeling of "There's never enough. There will never be enough." This drives us to feel hopeless and discouraged, which can lead us back to the old behaviors and feeling of deprivation that got us into trouble in the first place.

Meeting Needs Creatively and Inexpensively

Some needs can be met right away, and many can be met more simply than you think. One of the most startling realizations people have when they develop their list of needs is that so many of them can be met with little or no money. One woman with whom I worked listed *Time to relax and replenish* as one of her core needs. By stating it, she got clear that this need was important and deserved to be met. At that point, she did not have money for a long vacation. She was, however, able to plan a series of day trips on weekends to a nearby nature preserve that she loved. She satisfied her need for relaxation and replenishment for next to no money at all.

Evolving Needs

Needs are not static, unchanging things. Our needs evolve as we go through the various stages of our lives, when our circumstances change, or when sudden events occur. New needs arise as the more basic ones are met.

A good friend of mine has recently separated from her husband and lives alone on an isolated country road. She recognized that every night she was having difficulty sleeping and no longer felt as safe as she wanted to feel in her home. She had her heart set on having some beautiful landscaping done in her yard. Because her garden brings her great happiness and adds to the overall value of her home, landscaping falls into the *Need* category for her. She'd planned for this need and scheduled a landscaper to get started. However, when she acknowledged the degree of her new discomfort with living alone, a need for a home security system rose to the top of her needs list. This necessitated delaying the landscaping. The more pressing need upstaged the more optional one. To her, this security system was an important part of meeting her need to feel safe. Someone else might not feel this need, but she did. After having the security system installed, my friend slept better, was able to relax in the evening, and began to enjoy her country home again. Her relief was evidence that she had honored a need, and she had no regrets about postponing other, less pressing needs to meet it.

ADVERTISEMENTS: SMOKE SCREENS TO IDENTIFYING YOUR NEEDS

A discussion about distinguishing needs from wants would be incomplete without touching on the role of advertising and its impact on our financial lives. Ads bombard us constantly with messages about what we "need." What they really make us do is want everything.

There are overt ads, such as TV and radio commercials and print ads. Then there are product placements, which show our favorite stars drinking certain soft drinks or typing on computers with conspicuous logos. Athletes' uniforms are patchworks of sponsors' logos, and late-night TV is cluttered with infomercials, some hosted by tacky hucksters, others by dignified spokespeople. Product messages are coming at us all the time. Kids start asking for products by their brand names almost as soon as they can talk.

Advertising, along with the belongings of those around us, can be distractions, smoke screens that obscure our vision about what we really want and need. Ads make us feel that we need and want everything.

Why? Because advertisers are good at doing their jobs. They bait the hook, and retailers just have to sit back and reel in their catch. Those living with unmet needs and areas of deprivation are the perfect catch for advertisers because they are especially susceptible to their suggestions.

I'm a businesswoman. I have no desire to do away with a fair marketplace or the creative advertising industry that helps direct buyers to businesses — including mine. While I don't object to the existence of advertising and commerce, I strongly object to how passively we have come to experience it. Advertising is a constant noise to which many of us have become consciously deaf while our unconscious absorbs every message.

Here's the main thing to keep in mind about advertising: almost all advertising is designed to make you feel that you don't have enough of something, that the something you have isn't good enough, or that you aren't good enough without what they're selling. From Air Jordans to age-defying night creams, we are all tempted by the seductive ploys of advertisers telling us what we "need."

> I do not read advertisements — I would spend all my time wanting things.
> — FRANZ KAFKA

Caveat emptor is a Latin phrase that means "buyer beware." I think of it in another way. I say "buyer *be aware*." As you encounter the ubiquitous temptations of advertising, be aware of your real needs. Resist letting an industry tell you what is important to you. That's for you to determine.

THE SATISFACTION OF MEETING YOUR NEEDS

In the construction industry, when a house has been neglected for a while, contractors refer to the work required as "deferred maintenance." This means not that the house lacks window boxes filled with begonias or granite countertops but that the house's needs have been neglected. The plumbing is bad, the roof leaks, or the foundation is crumbling. The structure and value of the home are diminished because of these unmet needs.

When people first start the process of creating a healthy relationship with money, they often have lots of emotional and physical deferred maintenance. They may have been going without things they need for a long time. They may even have lost hope that they'll ever be able to have their needs met at all. Some of the neglected needs may be so enormous that they feel out of reach.

Right from the beginning of your Financial Recovery process, meeting your needs is essential, whether it's a need for a practical thing like windshield wiper blades or the subtler need to enjoy nature and solitude by taking a walk in the woods or on the beach. By identifying and meeting your needs you'll start to taste real satisfaction.

When a client tells me, "It felt so good to take care of that," I know that the person is describing satisfying a need and not just a want. Meeting needs feels good. It creates a sense of pride and hope. On the other hand, indulging wants by making purchases they can't afford often leaves people feeling guilty and empty. While it may take a while to repair your financial picture enough to perform all your deferred maintenance, taking care of the small things can give you a glimpse of what is possible.

> *This life is not for complaint, but for satisfaction.*
> — HENRY DAVID THOREAU

Small needs unmet can be like pebbles in your shoe, nagging you to take care of them. This could be the broken doorknob that falls off every time you open the door. It doesn't disrupt your life, but it's a constant annoyance. Meeting small needs prevents them from growing into bigger ones. By changing the oil in your car, for example, you'll spare yourself the far larger expense of repairing serious engine damage. Paying bills or filing taxes on time prevents late charges and penalties. When I spend money on meeting a need, especially when it is preventing bigger problems or higher costs down the road, it ultimately saves me time, energy, and money. This often means that over time I end up with more money to devote to things that are important to me. Then I can enjoy my purchase completely free of guilt.

Finding a sense of satisfaction by spending money on needs is an experience that is new to lots of people who go through Financial Recovery. For me, as for many of my clients, taking care of needs (after not having done so for a significant period of my life) gives me a great feeling of accomplishment. It's rather like parenting myself in a way that I was not parented. It might surprise you too that taking care of things like oil changes, broken doorknobs, or dental care feels deeply satisfying. Of course, who wants to buy weather stripping when they could use that money for something more fun? But what I now experience — and what I've witnessed in others who progress through Financial Recovery — is that when I take care of my needs in financially responsible ways, I have a sense of emotional satisfaction at the deepest level. It's a way of valuing myself and honoring my worth. Afterward, I feel proud for doing the nurturing and healthy thing, for taking care of myself. There's no buyer's remorse as there often is when I've spent impulsively. It's so much easier to walk without the pebbles of unmet need in our shoes.

CASE STUDY

Nelson

My client Nelson, a pharmaceutical rep, drove a car he considered to be a "classic." The problem with this classic car was that in addition to its frequent breakdowns, it had one profoundly annoying trait: it would no longer go into reverse. This necessitated that Nelson avoid parallel parking, garages, and virtually all other convenient parking solutions, which was especially challenging in downtown Seattle, where many of his clients were located. He had to drive around the area of his sales calls searching for a parking spot that he could both enter and exit without going into reverse. "Sometimes I'm late for appointments," he explained. He went on to describe the elaborate process that sometimes required that he push the car backward to get out of tough spots. "I really want a new car, but it's taking forever for me to save enough to pay for it, and it doesn't make sense to spend another nickel on that car." Nelson had his eye on a new Jeep Grand Cherokee SRT8 with four-wheel drive. He was an avid backpacker and skier who loved weekends in the Cascade Mountains, and the Jeep would be perfect for those excursions.

Nelson's making do without a fully functional car was an expression of his own feelings that he did not deserve to have this very basic need met. Nelson and I had explored issues of deprivation in his financial life and it seemed a good time to address the issue of the car. "Nelson," I said, "don't you think it's pretty essential to have a car that goes both forward and backward?"

I could almost hear the wheels turning in Nelson's mind. Finally he said with power and clarity, "It's embarrassing when I have to push it out of parking spaces, and I know it's costing me business. A car with reverse is definitely a need...but I guess a new Jeep is a want." I asked him if he'd like to continue deferring his need because the want was big enough and important enough to wait for. "No way," he said. "My car has been a pain for way too long. It might even cost me business. And my gas bill would probably go down if I had a better car."

That week Nelson used the savings he'd built up since he'd started Financial Recovery to pay cash for a used Subaru in nice condition with a good warranty. Not only could he use it on his business calls, but it was also useful for going to the mountains. "I really felt like a grown-up, taking care of my own needs that way," Nelson told me later. "It made me feel so much better about myself."

Two years later, after continuing to work through the Financial Recovery process, Nelson traded in his Subaru for a two-year-old red Jeep Grand Cherokee. He was thrilled. He paid cash and felt terrific about the purchase. "It was fun to fulfill a dream of mine in a financially responsible way," he said.

Sometimes a need is time sensitive. The pressing need for Nelson was a functional car. His dysfunctional "classic" car not only was an inconvenience but was hampering his daily function. Later, as his business grew more successful and his money management improved, his want of a Jeep stepped forward and became a need of a new, previously undiscovered kind. While the Jeep was an optional purchase — something that could be categorized as a want — it was a want that had lingered for years. It was not a whimsical, impulsive want. When Nelson was debt-free and could indulge this want in a financially responsible way, it filled him with a sense of pride and accomplishment — meeting an emotional need for achievement and self-esteem.

CLEARING THE WAY FOR YOUR DEEPEST DESIRES

As people continue working the Financial Recovery process, identifying areas of deprivation and discerning needs from wants, an amazing and intriguing thing begins to happen. They start to access deep desires that they may have never spoken about before or even known existed. Soon they discover buried dreams of buying a home, taking piano lessons, or learning about photography. Some talk of their fantasy of taking a sabbatical or learning about their family's roots by visiting the homeland of their grandparents. People begin wondering aloud about their dreams of starting a philanthropic foundation or taking time away from work to volunteer for causes they hold dear.

The progression of Financial Recovery begins to free your imagination. Once you are no longer living in survival mode, driven by unmet needs and deprivation, you start to examine with new eyes how you're spending your time, energy, and money. You can find options where you thought no options existed and possibilities where hopelessness always resided. You can allow yourself to imagine dreams that once seemed far-fetched or unattainable.

As you develop an ability to meet your most essential needs, the noise and distraction created by a troubled relationship with money are quieted. Without the deafening noise of worry, obsession, fear, and deprivation, you're able to hear and value that quiet voice inside that utters your deepest desires.

Desires are more than wants. Desires are longings for those things and experiences that enrich your spirit and feed your soul. Your desires are inextricably connected to your most dearly held values. Desires can be grand or small — philanthropic or just personally satisfying. They are reflections of the constellation of values, preferences, and dreams that are uniquely yours.

What happens along the course of creating a healthy relationship with money is not just about the external experience of money itself. The external changes start to influence deep, internal transformation. You become more intimately connected with your values and your spiritual and emotional essence. Emboldened by the small, daily successes of changing your money behaviors, you dare to dream of creating a values-based life that is beyond what you own and more about how you want to live.

In the beginning of the Financial Recovery process, when just making ends meet may seem barely possible, it may feel unfathomable that your deepest desires can become reality. But as you take your first tentative steps, then longer strides, on your journey toward developing a healthy financial reality, I assure you that what was once beyond your imagination will become possibilities, then realities for you to enjoy.

Setting a Firm Foundation

It's no accident that this chapter — focused on healing shame and deprivation, learning to distinguish needs from wants, and probing deeper to understand desires — precedes the chapters about the mechanics of money management.

Recognizing deprivation in all its forms and sorting needs and wants is a lifelong skill — and one I continue to work on to some degree every day. By beginning to heal our deprivation and learning to identify and meet our needs, we replace the destructive forces that drive our money behaviors with the healing and restorative forces of awareness, discernment, and intentionality.

The emotional part of this work — examining your relationship with money, exploring your needs, wants, and desires — becomes enormously powerful when you combine it with the mechanics of effective money management. Your internal insights and the external practices we'll discuss in the next three chapters form the solid foundation for your Financial Recovery.

CHAPTER FOUR

Getting on Track

*The Key to Becoming Conscious of
and Connected to Your Money*

The best mind-altering drug is the truth.
— LILY TOMLIN

*Putting off an easy thing makes it hard.
Putting off a hard thing makes it impossible.*
— GEORGE LORIMER

*N*ow that you have begun to address the emotional aspects of your financial life, it's time to move on to some of the practical how-tos of money management. You will not be abandoning the internal work, but will continue to weave it in as you learn the practical steps that will help you build the financial life you want. The emotional work and the practical strategies of Financial Recovery form the dynamic duo that makes this process so effective.

By tuning in to your money (both how it comes in and how it goes out) you will become conscious of and connected to it. The awareness you'll gain is the foundation for a healthy relationship with money.

BURNING OFF THE FINANCIAL FOG
AND RISING FROM THE MONEY COMA

There's a reason casinos make you turn your cash into chips in order to play their games. They may say it's for security, but there's a more profit-driven reason. If we were tossing real money onto the table, we'd play a lot differently. We'd be much more cautious. We'd have reasonable limits. If we couldn't afford to play, or decided that the pleasure of the experience didn't outweigh the possibility of loss, we might not play at all. When our money is in the form of colorful chips, however, we more easily become detached from its actual value. The chips become more like play money, and it's easier to be cavalier and throw out another blue or red one. Add a little alcohol to the mix and the casino has us right where they want us: in a financial fog where money is no longer money.

Unfortunately, many of us live in a financial fog even if we've never set foot in a casino. Let me clarify what I mean by *financial fog*. If you open your credit card statement and gasp because the balance is in multiples of what you thought it would be, you've probably been living in a financial fog. If you have no idea of your checking, savings, and retirement account balances, you've been living in a fog. If you keep stopping at the ATM because your cash seems to just disappear, you're in a financial fog. Perhaps you make note of the checks you write but ignore or forget about the automatic payments, debit card transactions, and ATM withdrawals you make. These practices, along with keeping only an approximate balance in your head rather than computing an accurate total, add to fogginess.

Modern conveniences make it even easier to drift into a financial fog. We use credit cards like chips in a casino rather than actual cash to pay for purchases. This distances us from the real consequence of our spending — the fact that we will have less money after we make our purchase. We order online. We buy with easy-pay plans that let us break down big expenditures into seemingly bite-sized pieces. Hey, it's only $59.95 a month! Never mind that we'll still be paying for that item years after we've sold it at a garage sale. Never mind that we have dozens of $59.95 financial obligations. ATMs spit out money as if by magic. When a friend told her kids that she didn't have enough money for a certain purchase, one of them looked up at her and said, "Just go to the money machine, Mommy. It never runs out."

When I was ignoring my bills, I was in a financial fog. I lived in a state of vagueness that was both a symptom of and a contributing factor to many of my money troubles. Like many of us, I was good at rationalizing and justifying my money behaviors. As a result, the situation got worse and worse until I was in a full-blown money coma. I was completely unconscious of my money behaviors and the negative impact they were having on my financial, emotional, and spiritual life.

If we've been in a financial fog or money coma for a long time, we might be afraid of emerging from it and seeing our financial life clearly. The 1960 Alfred Hitchcock film *Psycho* includes a scene in which a woman, portrayed by Janet Leigh, is brutally stabbed while taking a shower. After watching that gruesome scene, a lot of people found themselves pretty nervous about taking showers for a while. But if you watch the scene closely you'll see that the knife is never actually shown touching the woman's body. That's because Alfred Hitchcock knew that the images we conjure in our imaginations can be far more powerful than anything he could depict on the screen. On a similar note, when you're stuck in a financial fog or money

> *Self-delusion is pulling in your stomach when you step on the scales.*
> — PAUL SWEENEY

coma, your money problems can seem like a huge and formidable monster that grows scarier every day. Getting a clear view of your current circumstances and spending patterns might be very frightening, but until you look at them in the bright light of day, the situation only gets worse. Fear and denial are great monster food, letting the monsters of your imagination grow bigger and more dangerous — that is, letting your financial circumstances worsen. Fortunately, once you face your real financial picture, you can bring the financial bogeymen in your life down to size. With this clarity you can begin the process of banishing those money monsters forever and dissipating the fog in which they thrive.

TRACKING THE INS AND OUTS OF INCOME AND EXPENSES

One of the most important weapons to use against your financial bogeyman is *tracking*. Simply put, tracking involves noting all the money that comes in and all that goes out. Every time you spend or receive money, you will write it down, whether you're paying with cash, check, or a debit or credit card; whether you're receiving a check, an automatic deposit, or cash. For each expenditure, you'll need to record three simple things: the amount, to whom you're paying the money, and for what it was spent. For income, you'll note where the money came from, and the amount.

The idea of tracking what you spend might feel either daunting or impossible, but read on. Though people often resist it at first, they're shocked to see how this simple process begins to change their lives. When they start to track their money, people experience payoffs immediately. Just by writing down your transactions you are choosing to be aware. You are connecting to the experience of spending and to the impact of that spending as well. Many people find that by merely committing to track their transactions, they do a lot less unconscious or impulse spending. Tracking may seem like a very simple practice, but it will give you important feedback about your money behaviors as well as the chance to alter them. This is a big part of developing a healthy relationship with money.

While tracking means writing down every financial transaction, it's broader than just jotting down numbers. Tracking is a way of becoming and remaining mindful about your everyday interaction with money — not just how much you have, but how you're using it, how you're feeling about it, and the consequences of your money behaviors. Being disconnected from your money behaviors reflects being disconnected from yourself. It causes you to act in ways that contradict your own best interests. It sabotages your progress toward your goals.

Mikelann Valterra, author of *Why Women Earn Less*, trained to become a money coach at the Financial Recovery Institute in 1997 and today is a faculty member. She founded the Women's Earning Institute and is highly regarded as "Seattle's Money Coach." Mikelann became an instant believer in tracking, and I call her my "tracking zealot." Through her own experience and those of Financial Recovery clients, she has found that tracking is the linchpin of what she calls "radical financial clarity."[1] In *Why Women Earn Less*, she urges women to become radically clear, active choice makers in the details of their financial lives.[2] Of course, the same advice is equally valuable for men. Tracking is a way of telling yourself the complete, unvarnished truth about your money behaviors as well as acting with financial integrity. It is so freeing to be unchained from money deception on all levels. It's empowering to know that you are fully aware of your finances.

OVERCOMING RESISTANCE TO TRACKING

When I explain to clients that tracking means writing down everything that comes in and everything that goes out, I can almost hear the sound of screeching brakes. "Everything?" they ask, with a quaver in their voices. "You mean, I should track *everything*?" Smiles wilt. Bodies stiffen and hands start to fidget. Faces take on a look of panic. When this happens, I reassure people by reminding them that tracking just means documenting what's going on. Period. Some people have been hiding from the reality of their money for a long time, operating on principles of magical thinking, unrealistic hope, and denial. The thought of actually putting it all down in black and white can bring up such intense fear and shame that some clients nearly shut down. So strong is this resistance that there's a real risk of the Financial Recovery process stopping right here. Lots of people would sooner discuss their sex lives or show their plastic surgery scars than reveal how and where they spend their money.

If you have never tracked your spending or earnings, you're not alone. Many of my clients have never tracked their money prior to our work together. People tend to resist the idea of tracking more than anything else in this process. Below are some of the reasons and objections they state.

- It's too hard to track everything.
- I don't have enough time to track.
- That's too simple. It can't make that big a difference.
- I already do that in Quicken.
- I'll just write the big-ticket items. Little stuff doesn't matter that much.
- I keep track in my head.
- I check my balance online or at the ATM. The bank is way better at math than I am anyway.

- I don't like to think about money all the time.
- I'm just not a numbers person.

If any of these objections resonate with you and you are still feeling reluctant about starting tracking, ask yourself the question that TV personality and psychologist Dr. Phil McGraw has made famous: "How's that working for you?" If your answer is "Not so well," then tracking is a big part of the solution.

We resist tracking for lots of reasons. It's a change of habit, and most people find that changing behaviors can be hard — even when they really *want* to make the changes. When trying to make even small changes (keeping a tidier house, getting up a few minutes earlier to get to work on time, or committing to daily flossing) many folks find that they start out okay but slip back into their old patterns before long. However, when it comes to the seemingly simple change of tracking our money, our resistance reflects more than a mere reluctance to change. Even if we're experiencing excruciating pain about our relationship with money, it may be terrifying to take a good look at what's really going on with our spending, saving, and earning. Why? Because by tracking our money we may have to face uncomfortable truths about ourselves, our habits, and our behaviors as revealed by our spending and earning patterns.

> *Justifying a fault doubles it.*
> — FRENCH PROVERB

In some cases we hesitate to tell ourselves and others the whole truth about what we're spending because on some level we know that once we admit it, we'll need to make changes. We may know that our income doesn't support our eating out as often as we do or that we spend more on clothing or gifts than we know is wise. Deep inside, we might already understand that we can't really afford to provide as much support as we do to our adult children, that our home or car is more than we can actually afford, or that our retirement plans are not realistic. It can be hard to face these realities. We may feel guilty or embarrassed. We could be afraid that by tracking our spending, we'll be forced to make a change we don't yet feel prepared to make. We fear that our spending will be judged and that by revealing the amounts we spend on certain items we'll be "required" to give up things that we enjoy. But tracking is a tool, not a weapon for beating ourselves up. It's just information at this point. When you see this information, you'll still be the one to decide what works and what doesn't.

For some of us, money is where our secrets live, so tracking tends to reveal our secrets. These fall into two categories: things we're hiding from others and things we're hiding from ourselves.

Spouses and partners often don't want to reveal to each other how much they're spending on everything from beauty salon visits or Botox treatments to electronics or golf clubs. Many have long histories of hiding their spending. Countless women have told me they cut the price tags out of new garments before their husbands get home or pay only part of their hair salon charges with their credit card and the rest of it in cash. Women aren't alone in this, of course. Whether it's on clothing, gadgets, or entertainment, plenty of men also minimize or hide their expenditures from their partners.

Avoiding conflict can be another reason not to expose our spending behaviors to a spouse or partner. Rather than face the possibility that our partner might be angry or judgmental, we hide what we spend. The irony is that we can end up feeling ashamed for keeping secrets from the very person with whom we want to have the deepest, most intimate relationship.

Secrets are like mold. They flourish and grow best in dark places. The longer mold remains in the dark, the more pervasive it becomes. Ask yourself, "What might I be afraid I'll discover if I track my money?" Then ask yourself, "Is it worth becoming conscious of my spending and earning in order to have a healthy relationship with money?"

Single people are not immune to the issue of secrecy in spending. Married, partnered, or single, if we're invested in continuing a certain spending behavior, we might not want to let ourselves know what it's really costing. I've had lots of people (both men and women) tell me, "I don't really want to know how much I'm spending at the grocery store. I'd probably freak out." The fact that the freak-out would come from just *knowing* the amount that has already been spent indicates how guilty we might be feeling about our spending. People can feel this way about what they spend on eating out, clothes, shoes, entertainment, cosmetics — all sorts of things that they fear I'm going to "take away" or judge them for when it's revealed in their tracking. Again, tracking is just about becoming aware of your spending so that you can make thoughtful decisions about whether this is how you want to use your money. You get to decide.

Some people know — either consciously or somewhere deep inside — that their patterns of spending might illuminate other troubling or addictive behaviors, such as excessive eating, gambling, or drinking. For these people, Financial Recovery can be a bridge to healing other parts of their lives. You'll discover through tracking that *the numbers tell the story*.

THE SURPRISING BENEFITS OF TRACKING

Tracking gives us practical, real-life, and immediate information about how our money is coming in and exactly how we're spending it. Our tracking, and the awareness that comes with it, gives us information to create a realistic plan for our financial lives.

Every step of Financial Recovery is predicated on the reality of money without the shrouds of fantasy, magical thinking, and denial. When we're unconscious about our money behaviors, we can spend in ways that get us into emotional or financial trouble. But when we become conscious of our money behaviors by using tracking, the financial fog clears.

Money is the material from which your financial dreams will be made, but it is not a dream in and of itself. Tracking starts to take the dreaminess out of your financial dreams and turn them into realities. Becoming connected to your money behaviors by tracking will clear the financial fog and bring you back to consciousness from your money coma. You may discover that you spend money on things that don't really matter to you. This leaves you with less money to spend on things that are important to your quality of life and on things that meet your most important needs. While people are hesitant to track because of what they fear they'll have to give up, it is far more often the case that they get more of what they need and want by eliminating unconscious spending.

The purpose of money mindfulness is not to punish you for "bad" spending but to empower you to make informed choices about where your money goes. You get to decide. For Brian, tracking revealed a spending pattern of which he'd been unaware. Once he discovered it, he was able to change it painlessly and have more money for his family.

CASE STUDY
Brian

Brian owns an auto repair business. "My wife is way better with money than I am, so she manages the checkbook. It really stresses her out juggling the bills all the time. We make good money, but I'm pretty sure I could do a better job of managing what I spend."

Brian agreed to track both his cash and credit card expenditures. By tracking his cash, Brian discovered that he was spending hundreds of dollars each month in meals and drinks at Malloy's. "That's the sports bar near my shop," he explained. "I meet my buddies there sometimes after work and occasionally on weekends to watch games." He noted that he often picked up the tab for the whole table. "It's just a habit," he said. "You know, kind of a guy thing to do."

Because Brian had been using money drawn from his business account to pay for the tabs at Malloy's, his spending had felt invisible. In reality, he'd been reducing his household income by hundreds of dollars a month — an amount that would have improved his family's financial picture. He decided that going to Malloy's once a week was more reasonable and that he could enjoy weekend sporting events at home. He and his wife started hosting football potlucks on weekends with other families. This simple change made a huge difference in the family's finances. Brian still met his need for enjoying sports with his friends, but did so at a much lower monthly cost. In addition, the potlucks proved far more satisfying to him, and his wife and kids enjoyed them too.

So often, people find that the mere act of tracking their spending makes them think twice (or maybe three or four times) before making a purchase. As a result, they may make fewer impulse buys. Many people tell me something like, "I've been trying to eat less sugar, so I didn't want to write *Godiva Chocolates* in my tracker. Knowing I'd have to write it down helped me resist the temptation." The accountability created by tracking raises our awareness enough that we make wiser choices that are in keeping with all our goals.

The practice of tracking has become a ritual for me, and though I've grown a great deal in my relationship with money, tracking continues to keep me conscious of and connected to my spending. It remains an ongoing process. Knowing that I'm going to write down a purchase allows me the time to ask myself if I need to make it — if I *really need* to make it.

You may be thinking that tracking is only for those of very limited means — those who need to "mind their pennies." But some of the wealthiest people with whom I've worked have come to appreciate tracking. Rebecca is a Financial Recovery client whose assets are in the millions. She told me that people find it stunning when they see her tracking her spending. They assume that because she has so much money she doesn't need to keep track of it. Rebecca remains committed to tracking because it provides her with immediate feedback about her spending and acts as a barometer for her relationship with money. This consciousness lets her *choose* how and when she spends her money and on whom she spends it.

One of the biggest reasons that wealthy people lose their fortunes is that they are disconnected from their money. We've all heard of movie stars, professional athletes, or music idols who end up in bankruptcy. The amounts of money that those with great wealth have can feel infinite, and of course, this is simply not the case. Regardless of your means, tracking keeps you connected to your money in an immediate and ongoing way. Whether you are of wealthy or modest means, the ritual of tracking and the insights that it gives are the same. The commitment to tracking is not itself the goal. It's merely the path to the goal. Clarity is the goal. And clarity connects us to our spending and earning so that we can have a healthy, honest, and empowered relationship with money.

Time for Your Life and Other Bonus Benefits of Financial Clarity

I've noticed that as people gain clarity about their money, they gain clarity about how they spend their time and energy too. Many people come to realize that they have the same relationship with time and energy that they have with money. They always seem to end up not having enough time and energy, just as they end up not having enough money. They lose track of time the same way they lose track of money. They are depleted of energy just as they are depleted of money. Time and energy are important resources that require management and awareness, and often those who struggle with money management also struggle with time and energy management.

If you're not sure where your time goes, you keep spending it in ways you don't really want to, or you can't believe how fast it goes, you may be having trouble managing this resource. You're stunned when you find yourself exhausted when it seems there's still so much to do. You might be chronically late or perhaps you're running at warp speed all the time. It's exhausting. Tracking money often helps people to become aware of how they spend their time and energy too. The beauty of Financial Recovery principles is that they apply to the other areas of our lives as well. Donna was delighted to discover this for herself.

CASE STUDY

Donna

Donna is a single, working mom who usually felt as if she was running on fumes. By the time she got off work, picked up the kids, stopped at the grocery store, made dinner, and helped her kids with their homework, all she could do was fall into bed. When she described her vision of her ideal financial life, one thing Donna talked about was being able to take a Zumba class as a workout a couple of times a week and maybe even meet her girlfriends for dinner now and then. "It would be such a luxury to have that kind of time," she said.

When Donna showed me what she'd been tracking, I noticed something. "I see you go to the grocery store nearly every day," I said. We then figured out that it took Donna forty-five minutes to an hour for every store run and that the monthly grocery bill seemed fairly high for a family of their size. We devised a plan: Donna would write out a weekly meal plan on Saturdays; she'd do "big shopping" that day and go to the store once midweek for fresh produce and incidentals. After a month of following this plan, not only did Donna's grocery bill go down, but her family was eating more nutritious meals. The greatest payoff for Donna was that she found time for her Zumba class and an occasional dinner out with her girlfriends. A small reallotment of time and money let her meet these important needs.

Most people say they don't have time for tracking. In reality, tracking can help you save not only money but time and energy as well. Additional opportunities to save time and reduce the energy you waste fretting, finagling, and cleaning up financial messes will quickly become apparent.

Following are a few more bonus benefits to gaining financial clarity through tracking.

Insight into what's missing. Tracking often reveals areas of unmet needs, even areas of deprivation. This can help you devise ways to meet those needs — such as more time for yourself, pride in your home, or more social interaction.

Lower interest rates. Getting credit card and loan payments in on time will improve your credit rating. This means that if you choose to buy a home, refinance, or buy a car, you'll be able to get a better interest rate and thereby save thousands of dollars over the course of the loan.

Less clutter. As mentioned earlier, once people start tracking, they make fewer impulse buys, which results in less unnecessary stuff around the house. Also, as people identify their real needs and wants and begin to shape their spending to reflect what's important, they often start looking at their homes and closets with new eyes. The resulting "urge to purge" what's unnecessary leads to simpler, less cluttered surroundings.

Simpler tax prep. April 15th doesn't have to be a traumatic event. When you're tracking your money, it's substantially easier to prepare tax returns. You'll have documentation for legitimate expenses that you might have failed to deduct in the past. Again, it saves both time and money.

More free time. Like Donna, you may identify areas where you can save both time and money. Again, this awareness is all about giving you more of your resources and more choices about how to spend them. What could you do with a few extra hours a week?

Improved relationships. Many of my clients say that money is a primary source of family and relationship conflict. When you manage money through tracking, you may have fewer arguments about it. Also, tracking causes you to be more honest with yourself about money, which translates to more honesty in general, which promotes healthier communication.

REDUCTION OF STRESS-RELATED ILLNESS. If money is the source of stress and stress contributes to illness, doesn't it make sense that managing money better will contribute to your general health? In addition, if you've been unable to afford preventive healthcare, a gym membership, or fitness classes, being able to designate funds toward these will also contribute to better health.

INCREASED SELF-ESTEEM. Addressing something that you've been struggling with goes a long way toward building your confidence. Imagine feeling proud of your financial accomplishments and also knowing that you have nothing to hide — no secrets lurking behind a facade.

SPIRITUAL INSIGHTS. As you become more mindful in one area of your life, you'll become more mindful in others. Struggles can be a huge distraction from having the kind of spirituality you may crave. Money chaos can eclipse your view of your higher self, your higher purpose, and even your higher power.

WITH ALL THESE PERKS WAITING FOR YOU, don't you think it's time to start tracking? Let's do it.

THE SIMPLE NUTS AND BOLTS OF TRACKING

Developing the habit of tracking certainly takes a bit of discipline, but once you get it down it requires only about five to ten minutes a day. With this small time investment, you'll reap great dividends by staying in tune with all your money transactions.

To get started, you can decide whether you'd like to do tracking manually — that is, by writing your transactions in paper registers — or electronically. If you decide to track manually, you may use checkbook registers that most banks provide to their customers for free. To track electronically, you can use your smartphone or PDA or the web-based MoneyMinder Personal Money Management System I've developed. MoneyMinder is available for a modest fee on my website, Financialrecovery.com. I've spent years perfecting this program so that it's an ideal companion for the Financial Recovery process. In this system, you can easily create registers for all your accounts and, as you record, the math is done for you. Whatever method you use to track your money, doing it is what's important. The only way to do it wrong is *not* to do it.

Whether you track manually or electronically, I recommend starting with three types of tracking registers — one for cash, one for each checking account, and one for credit card transactions. Label each register to reflect the type of transaction it's for. Some people ask me if they can just record all their spending in one register. But it is important to track cash, credit card, and checking transactions separately. It sounds more complicated, but by separating these types of accounts, you'll remain mindful and keep yourself out of the financial fog. When you make a credit card purchase, for example, it doesn't immediately affect the amount of cash in your wallet or the balance in your checking account, so lumping the totals together would create confusion. The benefits of tracking each type of transaction are as follows:

- Cash Tracker: By tracking your cash, you will no longer wonder how that $200 ATM withdrawal disappeared so fast.
- Check Register: By keeping a running balance in your Check Register, you'll know exactly where you stand with

your account. You won't have to wonder if you're going into overdraft.

- Credit Card Tracker: By noting your credit card purchases as you make them, you'll be conscious of that invisible spending that, when unmonitored, can add up to a great big bill at the end of the month. Many people find that their commitment to writing down their spending helps them to reduce or eliminate many of their credit card purchases.

Every time you spend or receive money, write or type it in the appropriate register. This includes all income and other money that comes in, such as gifts, loans, or refunds. Where do you write income? If you're paid in cash (say, if a friend reimburses you for buying her lunch), you note it in your Cash Tracker. If you receive a check and deposit it into your checking account, note it in your Check Register. If you return items and receive a refund to your credit card account, make note of it in and keep a running tally in your Credit Card Tracker.

It's important to find a consistent routine that helps you record every transaction. Some people write or type the amounts of their transactions at the moment they make them, while others retain all their receipts and enter all the amounts at the end of each day or the following morning. It's also important to spend a few minutes each day totaling the balances in each tracker. This not only keeps you fully aware of how much money you have but also gives you immediate feedback about how your money behaviors affect the totals.

The habit of tracking sounds more complex than it is. Again, it requires only a few minutes a day. As you continue to practice, it becomes second nature and the real benefits emerge. Ask yourself, "Is my money worth my time?"

What Tracking Looks Like

Figure 4.1 shows a sample page of a Cash Tracker. Whenever I put money into my wallet, I enter it in the plus column. Note how simple the entries are while still including everything. If you do a good job of tracking your cash, you should be able to know exactly what's in your wallet by looking at your running cash total. If it doesn't add up, write *Unknown* as an entry in either the Cash In or Cash Out category. Not surprisingly, it's usually Cash Out entries that many people tend to forget. I tuck all my receipts into a special compartment in my wallet to make sure I have a record

FIGURE 4.1. CASH TRACKER

Date	Description of Transaction	Cash Out		Cash In		Balance Forward	
						35	12
3/6	Groceries	12	34			12	34
						22	78
3/6	Ice Cream	3	50			3	50
						19	28
3/7	Coffee	2	25			2	25
						17	03
3/8	Movie	7	00			7	00
						10	03
3/8	Popcorn & Coke	5	75			5	75
						4	28
3/10	Mary — reimburse for movie last month			10	00	10	00
						14	28
3/10	Unknown	3	20			3	20
						11	08
3/11	ATM			60	00	60	00
						71	08
3/12	Bus	1	00			1	00
						70	08
3/12	Newspaper	2	60			2	60
						67	48
3/13	Dry Cleaner	10	75			10	75
						56	73
3/14	Cab	13	00			13	00
						43	73
3/15	Babysitter	24	00			24	00
						19	73

of all my expenditures. Once I've entered these into my trackers, if I need them for tax reasons I keep them; otherwise, I throw them away. This keeps things clearer, and I avoid unnecessary clutter.

I have noticed that underearners tend to forget to note income. They may accumulate checks and fail to deposit them or neglect to charge for their services at all. Remember, tracking is the place where you become conscious of and connected to your money, whether you're spending it or receiving it.

Tips for Getting the Most Out of Tracking

The more you build tracking into your routine, the easier it will become. Many people pick up tracking right away and instantly see its value. They actually get excited by the practice of tracking, what it reveals to them, and how much more aware of their money behaviors they become. For others, the skill takes some time to build. The following tips will make it easier to get started and keep going with tracking.

SEPARATE DIFFERENT TYPES OF EXPENSES. One kind of spending can often disguise itself as another. When people have extraordinarily high grocery bills, for example, they might find that they're buying other kinds of items at the grocery store: toys, cleaning supplies, beauty products, dog food, or even cookware and kitchen gadgets. If you classify the entire amount as *Groceries*, you'll end up with a skewed notion of your food spending. Separate nongrocery items before they're rung up at the register so you can more accurately and easily track the types of items you buy. Or you can pay for the items together and then make note of the nongrocery items in your tracker.

DON'T RELY ON MEMORY. You might think you'll remember every transaction. Trust me; you won't. Memory failure and our natural tendency to downplay what we're spending can work together to get us off course. Tracking needs to become a daily ritual. If you wait until the next day, or the weekend, you are likely to lose track — literally.

WATCH FOR SNEAKY SPENDING TRICKS. People commonly commit tracking sleight of hand so they can resume old spending habits or hide expenditures that they feel will be judged in some way by themselves or others. Examples include asking for cash back from grocery store debit purchases or putting everyone's meal on a credit card and pocketing the cash they contribute. This is fine as long as you enter the correct amounts in your trackers. If you don't track such transactions, they will show up as exaggerated expenses while you're actually spending the cash in other areas. So if you get cash back from the supermarket or from friends after a meal, you will need to enter the credit card charge in your Credit Card Tracker *and* the cash received in your Cash Tracker.

Observe your money maneuvers. They can give you helpful information about yourself and your behaviors and habits around money.

DON'T LET THE QUEST FOR PERFECTION DERAIL YOU. If you find that you've accidentally forgotten to track some cash, figure out what's missing and enter it as *Unknown* in your Cash Tracker. Writing down $28 as *Unknown* is far better than scrapping tracking altogether because you can't track perfectly. Guess what? No one can. After a busy weekend, I often have small unknowns. I've forgotten buying ice cream cones for my grandkids or making small cash purchases at the farmers' market. No big deal. The important thing is that I notice the unknowns, and I know exactly how much they are.

Discovering unknowns in your tracking can provide you

with new areas of insight that can be just as valuable as noting what you spend. When we lose track of money, it often tells us that something more might be going on. Some people notice, for example, that they forget to note transactions when they are busy, distracted, stressed, or worried.

If you're on an all-day outing with your kids, for example, you might use cash to buy snacks, put money in the parking meter, get lunch, and buy balloons. You can keep it simple by entering *Outing at the Park* in your Cash Tracker and noting the total for the cash you spent. What's important is that you keep track of your cash transactions and keep a daily total, not that you spent three dollars on balloons. Keeping your tracking simple will let you enjoy the time you're spending with your kids even while you're staying in touch with your money.

If you get off track, don't be hard on yourself. Just get back on. If you miss a day of tracking, don't just throw up your hands and say, "Oh well, I guess that's over." Make your best estimates of your spending and turn the page. Tomorrow is another day, and you can start tracking all over again.

REMEMBER TO BE GENTLE WITH YOURSELF. When you're trying to build a new habit, you're bound to have lapses. I find that people want to quit tracking when they feel ashamed about a particular expenditure. Whatever you spend, write it down. It's all information that helps you on your Financial Recovery path.

STICK TO IT, EVEN WHEN AWAY FROM HOME. Lots of people go on vacation and decide to chuck their regular practices, including tracking. "I'm on vacation!" they say. "I don't want to think about money." Somehow the word *vacation* seems to translate as "I get to go berserk!" But how many of us have had a wonderful vacation spoiled by the debt that greets us when we get home? This is like waking up to a huge mess and a bunch of property damage after a lovely party. It ruins the whole experience. It's far easier to commit to tracking 100 percent of the time rather than deciding when to and when not to track. This includes tracking even when you're away from home. The quality of your vacation and its restorative value can be so much richer when you know that you are not doing yourself financial harm.

As I'VE SAID BEFORE, *the numbers tell the story*. Tracking is an important step to connecting to your own money story. It informs you of your habits and blind spots, and it can even begin to give you insight into how emotions play out in your relationship with money. This shines a great big light on your financial bogeymen — those monstrous fears and secrets from which you've been hiding. These become a lot less scary in the bright light of clarity that is achieved through tracking. Understanding your money monsters enables you to devise a plan to tame them. That's what we'll continue to do in the following chapters.

CHAPTER FIVE

Creating Your Personal Spending and Income Plan

*The Bridge from Where You Are
to Where You Want to Be*

*To get what we've never had,
we must do what we've never done.*

— **ANONYMOUS**

Luck is the residue of design.

— **BRANCH RICKEY**

M eeting your needs is at the core of every aspect of having a healthy relationship with money. Creating a monthly spending and income plan is the next step that gives you the practical tools for meeting your needs with the resources you have. This is where you'll really experience the *recovery* part of Financial Recovery. No matter your current circumstances, this chapter will help you create a specific and detailed plan that builds the bridge from the financial life you're living to the one you *want* to live.

Countless clients have told me how incredibly valuable creating a personal spending plan has been for them. It keeps them out of the financial fog and brings increased levels of clarity in their relationship with money. With a workable plan in place, people get excited and have less stress, knowing they'll make it through the month. An added benefit I often hear from clients is that it reduces arguments with their partners, so their personal relationships are improved too.

The monthly spending and income plan gives us a way of seeing the consequences of our choices *while we still have time to do something about them.* By planning your monthly expenses *before* you actually spend the money, you'll eliminate the vagueness that often accompanies living without a plan and the financial chaos that naturally results. A spending plan lets you be proactive rather than reactive — you'll no longer be forced to deal with every unexpected event and expense by just hoping that things will work out. By preparing for your expenses (even the ones that sometimes take you by surprise), you'll have the confidence of knowing that you'll be able to take care of them. You'll know ahead of time how your money will be used each month so that you can begin to meet those needs and areas of deprivation that you identified in chapter 3. You'll discover the clarity that comes with being really tuned in to your money and the confidence that follows. No more money monsters.

> *You've got to be careful if you don't know where you're going, because you might not get there.*
> — YOGI BERRA

You custom-design your spending plan to reflect where you want your resources to go. A good spending plan enables you to take care of your financial responsibilities, meet your needs, and enjoy life in the process. It helps you identify the things that bring you satisfaction and ensures that you get them. Over time, it will enable you to do things that may seem impossible to afford today.

It may be hard to believe, but designing and maintaining your spending plan can feel fantastic! After you've been at it for a while, you'll be amazed by how much a part of your life the process has become, and how satisfying and comforting it is to have a spending plan to guide your financial decisions. Keep the following factors in mind as you begin to imagine creating and maintaining a viable spending plan.

A good spending plan facilitates "Do No Harm" spending. At the end of movies in which there have been animal stunts, I often see the disclaimer "No animals were harmed in the making of this movie." That's how I like to feel when I've spent on something that is on my spending plan — "Karen was not harmed in the buying of this item." The goal of having a spending plan is to enjoy the peace and self-esteem that come with "Do No Harm" spending.

A spending plan is not a budget. To start the spending-plan process, you'll have to leave your old notions of budgeting behind. Spending plans are not budgets. Budgets usually feel restrictive. Budgets usually mean that you list all the bills you have to pay, then you get what's left over. Who wants to live on leftovers? The word *budget* is to money what *diet* is to food. Diets don't work, and money diets don't work, either.

A spending plan is not rear-view mirror accounting. Most people do what I call "rear-view mirror accounting." This means looking at the money they have spent after they have spent it. Their accounting is all about what has already taken place. There's no planning involved. They might do this at the end of a month, a few times a year, or even just once a year, at tax time.

While driving, no one would keep her eyes only on the rear-view mirror, never looking through the windshield at the road ahead. To be fully mindful about your money, you have to look forward too. You have to know where you're heading. A detailed spending plan is the tool that helps you look ahead and be prepared for what is in front of you, as well as what's around the corner.

CREATING YOUR SPENDING PLAN
ONE STEP AT A TIME

Below is an overview of the steps you'll take to create your own highly personalized spending plan. We'll go into specific details and examples to help you with each step.

Step 1. Gather needed materials
Step 2. Create your spending and income categories and subcategories
Step 3. Plan your monthly spending and income
Step 4. Determine "Will this plan work?"
Step 5. Make adjustments if necessary
Step 6. Stay connected with your plan
Step 7. Do a month-end review
Step 8. Create an annual spending plan

Of course, by definition, a plan comes *before* an event. This may be stating the obvious, but your monthly spending plan should be in place before the first of the month, every month. If you wait until later in the month, even just a few days later, most likely you'll have already spent some of your money, so you'll have less money available for your spending plan and therefore your spending choices will already be limited. (Of course, if you're reading this on the 5th or the 15th of the month, you don't need to wait until the end of the month to start working on your plan for the next month. Instead, you can make a plan for the remainder of this month. That way, by the end of the month, you'll be familiar with the process and better equipped to create a workable plan for next month.) Also, remember that each month is different, so you will need to update your plan every month. If you have a spouse or a partner, you might choose to create your plan together.

Over the twenty years that I've counseled clients, I've developed a fabulous tool, the MoneyMinder System, that provides you with everything you'll need for the steps listed above. It's available from the Financial Recovery Institute website (www .financialrecovery.com) for a modest fee. If you opt to create your spending plan yourself, you can use a simple Excel spreadsheet. These days, the vast majority of people use their computers to create their spending plans, but if you're more comfortable working on hard copy, you can use ledger sheets or even graph paper. The important thing is to find a system that works for you for planning your spending and income. Whether you prefer using the computer or pencil and paper, the point is to start right away in order to design a mindful and realistic spending plan that works for you.

Step 1: Gather Needed Materials

Here are the things you'll need to do to create your first monthly spending plan:

- Gather the bills that are due this month so you're aware of their due dates. Throw away any duplicate bills. This will reduce clutter and give you a clear inventory of what you need to pay out each month.
- Get your Cash Tracker, Check Register(s), and Credit Card Tracker(s). If you don't yet have any trackers or registers, then get your bank statements and credit card statements.
- Have a calendar to remind you of birthdays, special occasions, or events this month for which you may need to plan.

- Take out your Needs and Wants List so that you can remain aware of your unmet needs as you create your spending plan.

Last, create a comfortable place to work where you can feel relaxed and have the information from these sources at hand to help you more easily plan for your expenses and income.

STEP 2: CREATE YOUR SPENDING AND INCOME CATEGORIES AND SUBCATEGORIES

You're going to begin by creating a list of all the ways in which you spend money or generate income. Doing so will tell you a lot about how you live your life, what's important to you, and how to plan your spending to achieve the financial life you want. This list will become your spending and income categories and subcategories.

In the more than two decades I've spent going through this spending-plan process with people from all walks of life, I've had literally thousands of opportunities to refine the process of creating monthly plans that work. In that time, I've developed a pretty good idea of the types of expenses and ways of earning money that are common to most people. I've also learned just how important it is to make the plan personal to reflect each person's individual lifestyle, interests, and values.

The extent of most people's planning takes place on the back of an envelope or on a scrap of paper where they break their spending into broad, general categories like FOOD, HOME, UTILITIES, and so on. The problem with this is that it's so easy to forget all the other areas in which we spend money. We forget about the twenty we gave to our teenager for his lunch money, the dry cleaning that cost thirty dollars, and the new ink cartridge our printer needed.

Having main categories alone is not enough (this is where

most budgets usually stop). Having a plan with only main categories would be like driving cross-country with only a vague, general idea of where you're going and no details about the route you'll take to get there. By creating subcategories for both your spending and income areas, you will be personalizing the categories to suit your life. This will help you plan for and remember the lunch money, dry cleaning, and ink cartridge kinds of expenses that occur every month. Even if you use the categories I've created in the MoneyMinder System, you'll want to customize the subcategories to match your individual circumstances.

In order to think of the subcategories, brainstorm all the ways in which you spend money (or would like to spend money) to take care of your needs relating to that category. Looking at your trackers and/or your bank statements will help jog your memory.

Some of your subcategories will represent items on which you spend money every month, while others reflect expenses that crop up occasionally or seasonally. The latter are called nonmonthly, or periodic, expenses. Thinking about and planning for periodic expenses is one of the big keys to mastering your money. It's often these expenses that derail us, so by including them as subcategories, you'll be able to factor them into your overall spending plan. Whether it's car insurance, homeowner's insurance, property taxes, or holiday expenses, periodic expenses must be a part of any spending plan that will actually work. Rather than being thrown off course by these not-so-surprising surprises, you'll just experience them as part of what you encounter along the road.

Look at the month ahead on your calendar. Are there any birthdays, events, or appointments that will cost you money? Add any necessary subcategories. Review your Needs and Wants List as well. Is there anything on that list that you need to spend money on this month? If so, add it to your plan.

In order to make the steps of creating your monthly spending plan even clearer and to show you just how personal this process can be, we'll be using Susan, a Financial Recovery client, as an example for each stage of building a plan. While her circumstances may be different from yours, they'll give you an idea of how the process works. First, let's learn a little about Susan.

CASE STUDY
Susan

Susan is a single mom with two boys. At the beginning of this process, she was in financial crisis. She was working as a bank teller, struggling to make it through each month and using her credit cards to bridge the gap between her income and her expenses. After a painful divorce, Susan found that she often spent money on toys and other items because she wanted to make her boys' lives as happy and comfortable as she could. Meanwhile, she found that she was struggling to pay for rent, groceries, and other essentials. She realized that, instead of practicing "Do No Harm" spending, she was spending in a harmful way. It was time for her to have a plan.

Building a monthly spending plan was crucial to Susan's Financial Recovery process and to her sense of well-being. The way she'd been living was no longer working for her, and she knew she could not provide for the long-term needs of her boys without changing things. By simply thinking about her sources of income and the things she spent money on in any given month, Susan could determine what her main spending and income categories would be.

To get started, review the list of categories on pages 130–131. The descriptions of each can help you as you begin to think of subcategories that are specific to you. You may have additional categories not included on this list. Remember, you're making it personal.

To give you a feel for the process, next we'll explore some of the categories in detail. You'll notice that the order in which we're addressing main categories is not alphabetical, as it might be in lots of other budget programs. That's because this planning process is centered on what we've already covered in prior chapters: meeting your needs. Abraham Maslow listed shelter, food, and clothing as basic survival needs. It seems logical, then, to put home, food, and clothing among the first categories to address. However, notice that spiritual growth comes first. If you're wondering why, read on.

Spiritual Growth

This category includes any expenses related to nurturing your spirit. I have SPIRITUAL GROWTH listed as the first category on the MoneyMinder System. This is the first main category on a spending plan because for me, my journey with money has been a very spiritual one. This process has helped me dig deep within and discover the essence of how I am in the world — in ways that go far beyond money. Because money touches nearly every area of our lives, it provides us with an opportunity to learn about and express who we are and what's most important to us. Many Financial Recovery clients have discovered this for themselves too. Spiritual growth could include books, music, classes, and so on, as well as expenses such as donations to your place of worship. Figure 5.1 (see page 132) shows how Susan broke the category of spiritual growth into subcategories.

SPENDING PLAN CATEGORIES

SPIRITUAL GROWTH: This category includes any expense that is used to nurture your spirit and replenish you. It could include items such as books, music, classes, and donations to your place of worship.

HOME: Expenses related to having and operating your home, including rent, mortgage payment, home maintenance, utilities, household supplies, home or renter's insurance, property taxes, furniture, decorations, and so on.

FOOD: This includes groceries; breakfast, lunch, and dinner out; coffee and tea out; snacks and soft drinks; school lunches; and food for guests.

CLOTHING: Any category related to your clothing, including clothing purchases, dry cleaning, alterations, and shoe repair.

SELF-CARE: Expenses related to taking good care of yourself, such as personal care items and services, including haircuts, beauty treatments, cosmetics, and health clubs.

HEALTHCARE: These are the expenses related to your physical and emotional health, including health insurance, doctor and dentist visits, prescriptions, therapy, vitamins, and so on.

TRANSPORTATION: These subcategories will reflect your transportation needs, including gas, car insurance, maintenance, public transportation, tolls, parking, and so on.

ENTERTAINMENT: All expenses relating to things you do for fun and recreation, including social events (but excluding travel, which is a separate category).

DEPENDENT CARE: Subcategories associated with having children, elderly parents, or pets who are dependent on you.

VACATION/TRAVEL: These are the expenses for trips or vacations, including such things as airfare, accommodations, the money you spend on souvenirs, entry fees for museums and amusement parks, and the costs of boarding your pet.

GIFTS: All subcategories connected with spending for others, including charitable donations as well as personal gifts, greeting cards, and so on.

EDUCATION: All educational subcategories, including books and supplies as well as tuition and fees. (Note: You may want to account for some classes in other categories, depending on your purpose for the particular learning experience. For example, a cooking class might be a food expense for you, or you may take a class primarily for spiritual and personal growth.)

HOME OFFICE EXPENSES: The expenses for items you need to take care of personal business, such as postage, copying, computer supplies, and banking fees.

TAXES: Any expenses relating to your tax obligations, including not only direct tax payments but also the cost of accounting or tax preparation services.

INSURANCE: Personal insurance, other than those already accounted for as home, auto, and health insurance. Examples are life insurance, long-term care, and disability insurance.

BUSINESS AND PROJECTS: You may use this category if you have a fairly simple small business to account for, or special projects, such as a wedding.

SAVINGS AND INVESTMENTS: Any deposits you make to periodic savings, safety-net savings, and long-term/investment savings accounts (you'll learn about these accounts in chapter 6).

DEBT REPAYMENT: The amount you pay each month toward credit card bills and other debts, including loans from family or friends. Don't put mortgage or car payments here (these are already included under home and transportation). Be sure to list the names of each creditor separately.

INCOME: Include all income you receive in any form: paychecks, commissions/bonuses, gifts, tips, interest payments, dividends, child support/alimony payments.

FIGURE 5.1. SUSAN'S SPIRITUAL GROWTH
SPENDING CATEGORY WITH SUBCATEGORIES

SPIRITUAL GROWTH
Donations
Church/tithing
Seminars/workshops
Spiritual retreat
Meditation class

Home

Figure 5.2 shows how Susan broke the next major category, HOME, into subcategories that made her plan more specific. As you can see, the category of HOME includes expenses related to having and operating a home. You can see that Susan included CONTAINER GARDENING as a subcategory. She rents an apartment. Her only yard work is container gardening on her patio. If you are a home-owner, or if you have more space, you too might have categories related to gardening and lawn care. If you live in a rural environment, you could have septic or well services to list as subcategories. If you have a housekeeper, list that here as well.

Food

This is an expense category for everyone. How you break it down into subcategories will help you see exactly where your food dollars are going and how you feel about your relationship with food. Remember in chapter 4 when we talked about separating your non-grocery items from your food items? This is where you'll appreciate

FIGURE 5.2. SUSAN'S HOME CATEGORY WITH SUBCATEGORIES

HOME
Rent
Renter's insurance
Utilities
Telephone & long distance
Cellular phone
Garbage & recycling
Household supplies
Furniture/decorating
Container gardening
Linens/housewares
Bottled water
Laundromat

having done that. It will help you separate items such as household supplies and pet food from your food category. This way, you can get a realistic look at what you actually spend on food.

Figure 5.3 shows how Susan broke down this category into "bite-sized" subcategories. Notice that she included DRIVE-THROUGH RUNS AFTER SPORTS. Because she's the mom of two active boys, this is a common expense for her. It is useful to separate those drive-through runs from other food expenses so that she can see the precise impact this particular expense has on her

FIGURE 5.3. SUSAN'S FOOD CATEGORY WITH SUBCATEGORIES

FOOD
Groceries
Meals out — Susan
Meals out — family
School lunches
Fast-food takeout
Coffee/tea out
Snacks for the boys
Drive-through runs after sports

overall monthly spending plan. For you, a comparable expense could be dinner with your book club or daily coffee. However you customarily spend your food (and beverage) dollars will give you hints as to what your subcategories will be.

Entertainment

Susan's ENTERTAINMENT category breakdown appears in figure 5.4. It's especially important for you to plan for your social and entertainment needs as part of your spending plan. This includes all your entertainment expenses except for vacations and travel — I recommend that you have a separate category for travel expenses. Remember, this spending plan should reflect all aspects of your life, even the fun ones!

FIGURE 5.4. SUSAN'S ENTERTAINMENT CATEGORY
WITH SUBCATEGORIES

ENTERTAINMENT
Music/CDs/iTunes
Movies out
Movie rentals
Theater/concerts
Sporting events
Magazines/newspapers
Books/hobbies
Photography
Parties/holidays/guests
Girls' night out

Susan's subcategories reflect how she and her family take part in entertainment. For you, this category could include museum memberships or dance lessons. Whatever you regard as entertainment belongs in this category. Notice that Susan's plan includes a subcategory for GIRLS' NIGHT OUT. Staying connected with her friends is important to Susan, and it satisfies an important need. By including this in her plan, she was not only accurately planning her spending but also including her own needs as part of that plan.

Dependent Care

Because she's a mom, Susan's DEPENDENT CARE category includes expenses related to raising her kids (see figure 5.5). But in addition

FIGURE 5.5. SUSAN'S DEPENDENT CARE CATEGORY
WITH SUBCATEGORIES

DEPENDENT CARE
Boys' after-school care
School supplies
Sports equipment/uniforms
Summer camp fees
Healthcare
Boys' college funds
Matt
Allowance
Toys, books & video games
Electronics
Justin
Allowance
Toys, books & video games
Electronics
Cat food & supplies
Veterinarian

to all costs associated with having children, DEPENDENT CARE includes expenses related to caring for elderly parents or other dependent adults, pets, or anyone who depends on you. Notice that Susan got very specific about the expenses for each of her sons.

Debt Repayment

Our list on page 131 contains a specific category called DEBT REPAYMENT. Under that category you'll list the names of each of your creditors. We'll be discussing a detailed plan for crushing debt in the next chapter. For now, just list the creditors to whom you owe money, such as student loan, MasterCard, Sears card, and so on. Don't forget to include loan payments you make to family members and friends, and to itemize each debt separately.

Income

Last, you'll add INCOME to your spending plan. Separate your income into subcategories. Include all income you receive in whatever form: paychecks, commissions, gifts, tips, interest payments, dividends, refunds (such as tax or insurance refunds), and child support or alimony income. In short, include any money that comes to you. Some people tend to see cash tips and refund checks as "found money" and therefore don't feel the need to track them. But these sources of income could make a huge difference in how successfully your spending plan works for you.

YOU MAY HAVE NOTICED that some of Susan's expenses were not monthly expenses. Summer camp fees, for example, are not something she pays for every month. (Thank goodness!) This is a nonmonthly, or periodic, expense. Also, some of Susan's subcategories were placeholders. For example, she wasn't yet able to fund her sons' college savings account, but she wanted to see this DEPENDENT CARE subcategory every month to help her stay focused on it. Having a subcategory as a placeholder is a good way to keep such dreams alive so they eventually become realities. Again, your subcategories will reflect your personal expenses, needs, and way of life.

Now it's your turn. Let yourself brainstorm your list of spending subcategories using the list of categories on pages 130–31 as a starting point. Take some time with this. Think through how you spend your weekdays, weekends, and evenings. Be sure to consider the usual, and the unusual, expenses you encounter. Think of those nonmonthly/periodic expenses that have sometimes surprised you or sent you into financial panic in the past. Also imagine the categories and subcategories that you'd *like* to include in your spending plan, even if they seem unaffordable right now. Be as thorough and imaginative as possible, but know that your list doesn't have to be perfect. You'll have lots of opportunities to add categories and subcategories that you might have forgotten (or new ones you've never thought about) later. Remember, you're not putting in numbers yet. You're just creating the categories into which you'll classify your expenses and income.

I urge you to pause once you've created your list. Take a breath, take a break, take a walk, take a bath — whatever replenishes you and makes you feel rewarded. It's useful to take a break before going on so that you don't get overwhelmed. It's also really important to acknowledge yourself for every step you take on this journey.

STEP 3: PLAN YOUR MONTHLY SPENDING AND INCOME

You've gathered your materials (your records, trackers, and calendar), created your categories, and referred to your Needs and Wants List. You've created a comfortable place to work. Now the real fun begins — you get to go line by line, category by category, asking yourself what dollar amounts go into your plan. The way to do this is to look at each subcategory and ask yourself, "How much money do I think I'll need to spend on this category this month?"

Some amounts are fixed — always the same — such as your mortgage and car payments. Some amounts are variable — they change from month to month or season to season — such as utility bills, clothing expenses, and healthcare costs (and, for some people, income). Your periodic, nonmonthly expenses, such as insurance, taxes, and membership dues, don't occur every month, just occasionally. Therefore, some categories in your spending plan may be blank for this month. Every month, your plan will be slightly different from the previous or next month's. Because you will be working with this plan during the current month only, include only what you think you will spend and earn this month.

For some amounts, you may already have the bills in hand, showing exactly what you need to spend. For others, your trackers or past bank statements can give you clues. For still others, you'll be making reasonable guesstimates. Don't worry; it doesn't have to be perfect. This is just a start. After you've done this for a few months, your guesstimates will become more accurate.

In addition to estimating your expenses, you'll need to estimate this month's income as well. Your income may be the same every month, or it may vary. Under income, list all the money you anticipate receiving from any source in the coming month. This includes earned income, child support and alimony, eBay sales, rental property income, and so on. If you expect to transfer money from a savings account to your checking account, include that amount as well.

The number one objection I hear from people who are self-employed or on commission is that they can't do a spending plan because they don't know how much money they're going to be bringing in during a given month. But if they throw all planning out the window, they'll invite the same money disasters they've had in the past. In fact, if it's difficult for you to estimate your income, it's even more important for you to plan. Do your best to determine your income for the coming month by looking at all likely sources of income. You may want to estimate income conservatively to avoid being caught short. We'll talk more about planning your income for the month later in this chapter.

Now let's take a look at how Susan entered her estimates for spending on her monthly plan (see figure 5.6). The column on the right is where she entered the amounts she planned to spend in each subcategory that month. At the beginning, because she was starting with so many unmet needs and a large debt burden,

FIGURE 5.6. SUSAN'S SUBCATEGORY ESTIMATES
FOR SPIRITUAL GROWTH, HOME, AND FOOD

SPIRITUAL GROWTH	
Donations	10.00
Church/tithing	100.00
Seminars/workshops	
Spiritual retreat	
Meditation class	
TOTAL SPIRITUAL GROWTH	110.00
HOME	
Rent	950.00
Renter's insurance	
Utilities	85.00
Telephone & long distance	70.00
Cellular phone	49.50

FIGURE 5.6. SUSAN'S SUBCATEGORY ESTIMATES FOR
SPIRITUAL GROWTH, HOME, AND FOOD (*CONTINUED*)

Garbage & recycling	15.00
Household supplies	20.00
Furniture/decorating	
Container gardening	15.00
Linens/housewares	
Bottled water	
Laundromat	20.00
TOTAL HOME	1,224.50
FOOD	
Groceries	400.00
Meals out — Susan	
Meals out — family	25.00
School lunches	20.00
Fast-food takeout	45.00
Coffee/tea out	60.00
Snacks for the boys	15.00
Drive-through runs after sports	35.00
TOTAL FOOD	600.00

Susan had to create a rather bare-bones plan: she planned for less spending in certain areas than she would have liked. For example, although she loved eating out with friends, she acknowledged that it was more important to meet her and her sons' needs than to go out for dinner. Plus, she knew that if she were to eat at a restaurant, she'd have to charge the meal, so she didn't put the cost of eating out into her spending plan. Instead, she told herself she'd make delicious meals at home and invite friends over occasionally. Over time, she was able to expand her spending plan, but we'll find out more about that later.

Now it's your turn. Follow Susan's example to fill in the estimated monthly amounts on your personal spending plan.

BEFORE GOING ON TO THE NEXT STEP, take a moment to pause and notice how you are feeling. At this point, seeing their expenses and income all laid out in front of them, people frequently feel a bit worried that their plan won't work. If you're feeling that way, take a deep breath. Just breathe a few moments before reading on.

STEP 4: DETERMINE "WILL THIS PLAN WORK?"

This is where it all comes together. When I come to this step in my work with clients, it's sometimes challenging for them, and it may be for you too. Again, breathe. It helps to know that at this point your spending plan can still be changed. It might not yet be a workable plan. That's what we're finding out. If your expenses exceed your income, the next step will help you adjust your plan so that it does work.

If you are using an electronic spreadsheet or the Money-Minder System software, the math will be done for you. If you're working in a hard-copy format, you'll make these calculations:

1. Total the amounts in each expense category.
2. Add together all the totals from all the expense categories.

3. Total the amounts in your income category.
4. Subtract the total expenses from the total income.

Your job now is to answer the question, Will this spending plan work? If you get a positive number when you subtract your total spending from your total income, it's likely that you have a workable plan. This is great! It's also possible there are some expenses you've forgotten about. This is common. And even if your plan appears workable, you may still want to make adjustments, which we will address in step 5. One of the things you'll need to consider is that if you don't get paid until the 5th of the following month, you'll need enough money left at the end of this month to cover your expenses until your paycheck arrives.

If your estimated expenses exceed your income or if you don't have enough to go into the following month, it can be very uncomfortable to face. Many of us have a history of feeling as though there will *never* be enough, and we're vulnerable to getting discouraged here. Don't worry. The process does not stop here. If your plan doesn't yet work — in other words, if your expenses exceed your income — the amazing creative process of making adjustments is right ahead of you in step 5.

Remember, the solution to a plan that does not yet work is not to pull out a credit card to make up the difference between your income and your expenses. That only makes things worse and deepens your debt load.

Susan's first-draft monthly plan did not work. Her expenses were greater than her income. This was important information for her — it told her exactly why using credit cards had begun to feel like a necessity just to make ends meet. It took some work, and she had to make some choices, but by going on to the next step of this process and making adjustments to her plan, Susan was able to create a plan that worked for her and for her boys. She felt hopeful for the first time in a long time.

STEP 5: MAKE ADJUSTMENTS IF NECESSARY

Please don't get discouraged if your spending plan doesn't work the first time through. This is very common, especially when you are just beginning. Knowing your shortfall at the beginning of the month is really important because *you still have time to do something about it!* Now is the time to adjust your expenses and income and create a livable plan for the month ahead. This is your opportunity to tap into your creativity and do some problem solving.

This is where I say to clients, and now to you, that I know how you feel — I've been there too. What I've experienced, personally and professionally, is that this process works. You can trust the process. I can't tell you how many times I have worked with clients who started out feeling, "Why bother? This is the way it always is. There is never enough." But in every case we found a solution by going through this adjustment process. It worked for them, and it *will* work for you. The adjustment step is where you get very focused and creative about how you're going to create a plan that will work just for this one month.

When your income isn't enough to cover your planned expenses, there are two basic questions to ask yourself:

1. Can I reduce my expenses? and
2. Can I bring in more money?

We will look at each of these questions in turn.

1. Can I Reduce My Expenses?

Remember all those subcategories you created? Your subcategories are where you'll reduce your expenses. You'll need to go through your plan line by line, category by category, to see if you can discover expenses that can be comfortably adjusted or eliminated this month. With each expense, you are going to ask yourself, "Is there a way I can meet this need for less or no money?"

People are often tempted to erase certain categories or subcategories from their plan. But if you start slashing away and erasing categories, you run the risk of re-creating the very state of deprivation that may have caused your financial problems to start with. The adjustment process is not a process of elimination — it's a process of exploration. You'll be exploring ways to meet your needs and honor your responsibilities for less money, instead of eliminating them. Also, if you make your plan so strict that it's unrealistic for your lifestyle, you'll just quit the planning process. This is why so many other financial programs fail.

You know exactly how much your shortfall is because you found that in step 4. As you look at each subcategory, rather than just eliminating an entire section, ask yourself if you can meet that particular need in a way that costs less or no money. You'll want to spread these adjustments over several categories so that you keep the integrity of your plan intact.

Some categories, such as your rent or mortgage payment, can't be adjusted, but many others can be. Making an adjustment could mean renting DVDs instead of going to the movies. It could mean having a potluck with friends instead of eating out. If you spend a lot of money on books, take advantage of your local library as a free alternative or arrange to swap books with friends. While you might prefer not to have to make these adjustments, you can make them willingly because it helps you go into the month knowing that you have a plan that will work.

As you review your expenses to make adjustments, look at your expenditures with new eyes. Ask yourself about the needs, or even simple habits, that might be driving your expenses beyond your ability to meet them. For example, if you and your partner have a ritual of going out for breakfast on Sundays so that you can enjoy time together before starting your busy workweek, this would be a subcategory; you'd note it under FOOD as BREAKFAST OUT. Of course, doing this weekly adds up. The question to ask yourself would be, "Can I meet this need by spending less or no money?" One possibility would be to reduce the expense by going out two Sundays a month. The other two weeks, you could perhaps enjoy cooking breakfast at home and reading the Sunday paper together. It might be just as satisfying to have a relaxing breakfast at home. In other words, if your real need is to relax and spend time with someone you love, you can meet it for substantially less money or none at all. Notice that I did not say cut out the need. If you're looking forward to this comfortable tradition with your partner, don't eliminate it, or you'll feel deprived.

You could also notice that you spend a great deal buying lunch each workday. It might be reasonable to consider bringing your lunch a couple of times a week to adjust this expense. However, I caution you not to make an all-or-nothing decision such as, "I'm going to brown-bag it every day, and I'll bring a Thermos of coffee from home." If you have been buying lunch and coffee every workday, it's not likely that such a radical vow will stick. It's better to be realistic. Perhaps you can bring a lunch two days a week. This alone will trim your expenses, but in a way that is doable and realistic. You want to make sure that the adjustments you're making are ones to which you can truly stick. That will give you a plan that really works.

Making adjustments to your spending plan requires creativity, but make sure that your creativity improves your circumstances. You'll want, for instance, to resist the trap of deferring monthly bills to make your plan work. If you put off paying your utility bill, for example, it will only cause the next month's bill to be that much bigger and more difficult to manage. If you keep doing this, it will result in late fees. This might help in the short run, but it will eventually (sometimes very soon) result in a monthly plan that doesn't work as well as adding more debt.

Sometimes, if you've had unpaid bills for a period of time, it might not be possible to pay the whole balance in one month without creating serious deprivation in other areas of your plan. At this point, you may need to call creditors or utility companies to arrange a payment plan. With your spending plan in place, you'll have an idea what you can afford to pay each month. This will help as you negotiate a realistic payment plan with creditors.

Let's consider Susan's plan again. When she subtracted her estimated spending from her estimated earning, she arrived at a negative number. Rather than scratching subcategories from her plan, Susan got creative and explored areas in which she could reduce spending without leaving needs unmet. Figure 5.7 shows Susan's adjustments (amounts in parentheses represent deductions). She looked to her ENTERTAINMENT category. Rather than paying for movies and movie treats, she and her boys decided to make every Friday "movie night." They borrowed DVDs from the public library, so their movies were free. They popped their own corn and brought sleeping bags into the family room to enjoy the show. "The boys love movie night," Susan explained. "It costs almost nothing and it's really fun. It's something they look forward to every week." Notice that she did not go without meeting the need for entertainment and for spending time with her sons. In fact, I think the real need was more deeply met after the adjustments. As you continue to use your creativity to make your plan work, you may find, as Susan and her sons did, that the alternatives you discover turn out to be better than what you're used to doing.

Now go to your spending plan. Go down item by item, category by category, making adjustments wherever possible, entering those adjustments in the ADJUSTMENT column. For instance,

**FIGURE 5.7. SUSAN'S ENTERTAINMENT CATEGORY
WITH ADJUSTMENTS**

ENTERTAINMENT	Initial Plan	Adjustments	Adjusted Plan
Music/CDs/iTunes			
Movies out	33.00	(22.00)	11.00
Movie rentals	10.00	(5.00)	5.00
Theater/concerts			
Sporting events			
Magazines/newspapers			
Books/hobbies	20.00	(20.00)	
Photography			
Parties/holidays/guests			
Girls' night out	50.00	(15.00)	35.00
TOTAL ENTERTAINMENT	113.00	(62.00)	51.00

under the main category of FOOD, you might adjust your LUNCH
OUT subcategory. If you had entered $100 and you decide you can
instead spend $50, you'll enter –$50 in the ADJUSTMENTS column.
You may not be able to make adjustments to every subcategory in
your plan, but you may be surprised by how many subcategories
you *can* adjust while still ensuring that your needs are met.

2. Can I Bring in More Money?

So far, we've been looking at adjustments in spending categories. Now it's time to look at your INCOME category. This is

where people's ingenuity and creativity really shine. They come up with creative ways of generating money. People sell items on Craigslist or eBay or take items to consignment stores. I worked with a musician who had a massive collection of music CDs that he no longer used. Many were collectors' items. He supplemented his income for several months by selling his collection and found it really satisfying to bring in more money. Some people even remember that other people actually owe them money! Other people decide to pick up a little overtime or help a friend with his catering business for a weekend or two. The added work can be temporary and doesn't have to become a way of life, but it can help you dig out of the hole and get yourself a plan that will work.

Once you've gone through your plan, making adjustments where you're able, you are going to figure out the effect of the adjustments you made. Total each expense category's adjustments, then add up the adjustments from all the expense categories. This is how much spending you've deducted from your plan. Then add up the adjustments you've made in the INCOME category. If these two figures combined match or exceed your shortfall, then you've got a successful spending plan. This plan will work!

Sometimes, it takes more than one go-round. If you go through this entire adjustment process and it still doesn't result in a plan that works, take a breath and go through the process again. It's not always easy to make substitutions and adjustments, but it's easier when you keep your larger goal in mind. It might be challenging, but doing this process will ultimately result in a great feeling. You will have a plan that works!

Susan had long allowed guilt to guide her purchases for her sons to compensate for their dad's not being in the picture. She felt guilty for having to work long hours. She overbought toys, spent lavishly on vacations, and basically never said no. She had done all this at the expense of her financial security. Worse yet, she wasn't happy with the financial role model she was providing for her sons. During the course of her Financial Recovery, Susan discovered the real difference between needs and wants, and devised a spending plan that helped her live the financial life she wanted to model for her boys. She discovered the real benefit of a spending plan: instead of spending money in ways that don't have a positive impact on your life, you can choose to trim back on inadvertent or habit spending in order to get the things you truly need.

As you work through the process of creating and adjusting your spending plan, it's natural for emotions to surface. You may feel frustrated by having to delay gratification. You may feel angry or embarrassed that debt you've created is constraining your available funds so much. Some people are actually surprised by new feelings of hope about their financial picture. Whatever your emotions, they can be important tools that help you recognize your true needs and make the best choices for how to use your money to meet them. And once you go through the adjustment process, you will know you have a workable plan. You are going to start the month knowing that if you stick to this plan, everything will work out. Imagine how great that's going to feel! A workable monthly spending plan might just be the best present you can give to yourself.

After working with your plan for a while, you will be happy to discover that not all adjustments are negative. After she'd been using her spending plan for about eight months, Susan and I looked at it to see what might be missing and what needs she still might need to meet. "What I'm really missing is time," she said one day. Susan's busy workweek and evenings filled with homework and cooking dinner left her exhausted. She spent Saturday mornings catching up on household tasks like cleaning and laundry, and she felt as though she didn't have as much time with the boys and for herself as she'd like.

At this point, she was stable on her bills and was no longer paying late fees and penalties on her credit cards. She'd begun to save and was making consistent payments on her debt. By eliminating a lot of impulse buys, she'd been able to see that she actually had enough to live on — and a little more. "Let's see how you can buy yourself some time," I said. "If you had someone come in for four hours every other Friday to clean and do laundry, that could free up your Saturdays," I suggested.

"But can I do that?" she asked. "It seems like such a luxury."

Susan and I discussed what the word *luxury* meant to her. By the end of our talk, she had redefined getting some help so that she could relax and have time with her sons as a need. As a single parent, Susan hadn't imagined she could ever have any help in caring for her home. She'd assumed she was always going to be on her own, tending to these tasks herself. Finding a way to buy some time within the scope of her spending plan felt heavenly, and Susan decided to fully enjoy it.

STEP 6: STAY CONNECTED WITH YOUR PLAN

Now that you've worked hard to create this plan and made adjustments so that it will work, it's important to stay connected with it throughout the month. Your spending plan will work only if *you work it* on an ongoing basis.

Staying connected to your spending plan throughout the month is the way to keep your plan going and end the month the way you intended. You wouldn't start that cross-country trek by looking at a map once and just driving, hoping to stay on track for the whole trip. In order to ensure that you'll arrive at your chosen financial destination, it makes sense to consult your spending plan regularly to stay on course. This allows you to make changes along your route if something unexpected happens. By checking your progress along the way, you get these benefits:

- You can see how closely your actual expenses fit with the plan you made. It's not unusual to have expenses you didn't anticipate or in different amounts than you estimated. This is not failure on your part, just information. (By the way, sometimes things cost less than you estimated.)
- You can make any needed adjustments if you find that your expenses exceeded what you planned. You can make sure that you don't have shortfalls as the month progresses.
- Perhaps most important, you get the security of knowing your progress and alleviating that out-of-touch feeling that comes with being disconnected from your money. You stay out of the financial fog!

Checking in with your plan also lets you see if income is coming in as you'd planned. This is particularly helpful for those who are self-employed or work on commissions that could fluctuate, but it's useful for those who receive a salary as well.

Occasionally you may have the happy surprise of more income than you anticipated. Whether it's an unexpected bonus, a gift, or extra earnings from overtime hours, more income gives you a terrific opportunity. When a little extra income arrives, people often make the mistake of thinking, "Hey, let's go get a new TV." My suggestion is to first go back to the areas in your plan where you made adjustments and allocate more money in those categories. Here's your chance to readjust your adjustments and meet any unmet needs you might have. Remember, the ultimate goal of Financial Recovery is to meet unmet needs and heal your areas of deprivation.

Recording Your Actual Expenses and Income

One of the most important ways of staying connected to your spending plan is through recording. Recording means taking the information from your trackers, every day, and entering it into your spending plan. This will let you know whether you still have money available to spend in your categories. It keeps you mindful of what's gone, what's left, and how you're doing.

Some people record all money in and all money out at the end of each day. Others enter it every morning, recording what they did the previous day. This is a great way to begin the day. It takes only a few minutes to look at your trackers and then record on your plan the amounts you actually spent. Many people grow to love this part of the process, as it helps them get better and better at identifying possible adjustments they can make to meet their needs for less money. If they've gone over in a category, or they see categories where they'll spend less than they'd anticipated, they need to continue making adjustments. Remember, you always want to be able to answer yes to the question, *Will this plan work?* Staying connected is how you ensure that the plan works, and keeps on working.

Figure 5.8 shows the FOOD category of one of Susan's early monthly spending plans. To the right of the ADJUSTED PLAN column, she recorded the actual amounts of her spending and income for each subcategory on each day of the month. (Figure 5.8 shows the amounts only for days 1–9 of the month, but her actual plan includes a column for every day of the month.)

FIGURE 5.8. SUSAN'S SPENDING PLAN RECORDING FOR FOOD, DAYS 1–9

FOOD	Month Plan	Adjustments	Adjusted Plan	1	2	3	4	5	6	7	8	9
Groceries	400.00		400.00		127.56			15.85				82.64
Meals out — Susan												
Meals out — family	25.00		25.00									
School lunches	20.00		20.00					5.00				
Fast-food takeout	45.00		45.00									
Coffee/tea out	60.00		60.00	3.15	3.15	3.15	3.15	3.15	3.15		3.15	3.15
Snacks for the boys	15.00		15.00				3.25	3.25				
Drive-through runs after sports	35.00		35.00	5.25				5.25				5.25
TOTAL FOOD	600.00		600.00	8.40	130.71	3.15	6.40	32.50	3.15	0	3.15	91.04

Challenges of Staying Connected

As you continue to use your plan throughout the month, it will evolve and unfold. You may experience some challenges that tempt you to abandon your spending plan. Anticipating potholes on any road can keep you from having a blowout. Anticipating challenges that are natural parts of any road to Financial Recovery can help you stay on your path and arrive safely where you want to go. Let's look at a few of the most common challenges.

INTERNAL RESISTANCE: It's natural to experience resistance when you're trying to build new habits. Resistance can show up as negative self-talk, as in, "This will never work. I never stick to things." Resistance can also take the form of focusing only on the negative experiences of the past, rather than the possibilities we can create.

In the day-to-day, you may find that you feel resistance to tracking expenses or recording them on your spending plan, particularly if you're embarrassed by the expenditures. For example, if you're struggling with weight issues, it may bring up feelings of shame to record that you're spending money on snacks. People concerned with their habits of smoking or drinking too heavily can also be reluctant to note expenses for alcohol or cigarettes. Even though it can be uncomfortable to look at our habits in black and white, doing so reveals the consequences of our money behaviors, and the discomfort that results could serve as impetus for further change.

Remember, small changes add up over time and serve to transform your entire relationship with money, and perhaps other areas of your life as well.

SELF-SABOTAGE: If you've been accustomed to a life of financial precariousness, it might feel strange to be financially stable. Functioning in survival mode consumes a lot of energy, creates drama, and provides enormous distraction. Some people find that it feels uncomfortable to feel comfortable. For those whose backgrounds have included neglect, abuse, trauma, or a lot of up-heaval, stability can feel really unfamiliar. The chaos has served as a distraction from emotional issues that run deeper than money problems.

I've counseled people who work earnestly to re-create their financial lives. Then suddenly they sabotage their efforts by either going on a spending spree or neglecting to pay bills, even though the money is available. They stop tracking and chuck their spending plan, even though it was working. It's as if they just can't tolerate things going so well or can't get rid of their money fast enough. Sometimes a particular stressor, such as a conflict with a mate or the death of a loved one, triggers episodes of sabotage, but other times it seems to come out of the blue. However, when we look closely we can often recognize the signs that a self-sabotage event was on its way: frustration, anger, stress, relationship conflicts, loneliness, isolation, fatigue, worry, or feeling unappreciated.

Self-sabotage is so common in Financial Recovery that it's worth it for all of us to try to anticipate it. By so doing, we might just be able to prevent it or get right back on track when it happens. This is about getting conscious of and connected to not only your money behaviors but your emotional experiences of money as well.

PERFECTIONISM: A spending plan develops organically. It will grow and change as you do. It will become more sophisticated and precise as you become more aware, skilled, and knowledgeable about your financial life. Sometimes your actual spending will match your plan. It will be "right on the money." Other times there will be differences between what you plan and what you

> *A man's errors are his portals to discovery.*
> — JAMES JOYCE

spend. That's all part of the learning curve. You'll learn as much from these differences as you do from your accurate predictions. Even with variations, having a flawed plan is an enormous improvement over not having a plan at all. View any variations as feedback, not failure.

THE "OH WELLS": The most common reason that spending plans fail is what I call the "oh wells." This is when we resume impulsive buying, stop tracking, or rationalize to allow for spending that is not in keeping with our design. We tell ourselves, "Oh well. It's just a small amount, and I deserve it," or "But this is such a great buy, I just can't pass it up. Oh well."

Sometimes the "oh wells" occur when uncomfortable feelings arise and we resort to old spending behaviors to soothe ourselves. Sometimes we drift into "oh well" behavior when we are under stress, undergoing change, or just tired of being so conscious of our money all the time. The "oh wells" are a very slippery slope. Once we start, our shame, guilt, or frustration with ourselves can kick in and we can slip right from the "oh wells" all the way into the "what the hells." That's when we can do some real damage. Many times we slip into this behavior because we were too drastic in our cutbacks and sent ourselves into feelings of deprivation. Rather than finding a moderate way of meeting our need, we just flip back into our old, overspending ways.

> *Beware of little expenses: a small leak will sink a great ship.*
> — BENJAMIN FRANKLIN

Some people find that certain places or people stimulate "oh well" thinking. Avoiding the people, places, and things that trigger destructive spending habits can help. For some, this means limiting shopping experiences. If you've been an overspender, shopping might have been your social recreation and your entertainment. Wandering through a mall can be to an overspender what walking into a bar is for an alcoholic. It's just too tempting and not worth the risk. Also, it is usually a good idea to either shop alone, with your specific list in mind, or to shop with someone else who will support you in sticking with your spending plan. Sometimes the social shopping trip ends up with everybody spending more money. Many people find that they can manage shopping much better if they bring only the cash they have available for the items they intend to purchase and leave credit cards at home. This keeps them mindful of how much they're spending and reduces the likelihood that impulses will take over.

As an example of a place that can cause people to get off track, a friend of mine recently told me that she and her husband "can't afford to save so much money at Costco." I laughed because bargain stores and sales are designed to make you feel as though you're saving money, getting a deal. You can use discount stores and warehouse shopping to your advantage if you go with a list and stick to it. If instead you go into these huge warehouse stores and see a football field full of bargains you can't resist, you might consider staying out of these stores at this point in your Financial Recovery. If you do go, take your list and only the cash you have in your plan for the purchases you've already determined. This approach will help your financial program work.

ANTICIPATING THE CHALLENGES that could cause you to abandon your spending plan is crucial to making Financial Recovery a way of life, rather than just another tried and failed attempt to change your relationship with money. If you find it particularly difficult to overcome these challenges, then getting support from a Financial Recovery counselor or qualified money coach can give you valuable assistance in staying connected to your plan.

Step 7: Do a Month-End Review

Doing a month-end review is the process of comparing what you planned to what actually occurred with your money during the month. This step lets you use your spending plan as a tool for self-discovery. Comparing your planned to your actual spending and earning helps you gain clarity about how the spending-plan process works. This is an opportunity to get to know yourself better and to gain skills that help you create your spending plans even more effectively.

While it's important to review your progress at the end of the month, don't let yourself get discouraged when reality seems to bear too little resemblance to your plan. Again, this isn't failure, only feedback. Over the course of just a few months, you'll find that your skills will grow and your estimates will prove more and more accurate. Most important, you'll get connected to exactly what behaviors pull you off course. Over time, this will help you recognize and alter self-defeating behaviors before they happen.

When Estimates Don't Match Actual Expenses

At the end of the month, you'll determine how closely your planned amounts were to your actual spending and income during the month. Sometimes your planned amounts don't match what actually occurred. (If you stay connected to your plan along the way, this won't be a surprise, and you may have made modifications to your estimates as the month progressed.) When your projections for a particular category differ from your actual spending, it's usually for one of the following three reasons:

1. You're not yet sure how much to allow for certain expenses. This could be because you didn't know the cost of certain items or because you haven't been tracking your expenses long enough to make accurate estimates. This is

a normal part of the learning curve, and you'll get more
skilled each month that you use your plan.

2. Something happened that you could not anticipate. Perhaps an out-of-town relative fell seriously ill, and you
had to travel unexpectedly. Circumstances beyond your
control will happen from time to time, and they can disrupt even the most carefully constructed spending plan.
This is why it's so important to have savings. Even a small
savings account will help you to keep your financial life
stable. We'll go into how to create and use savings in
chapter 6.

3. You spent impulsively without consulting your plan or
considering whether you could afford the expense. This
is the most challenging part of sticking to your plan,
because it requires that you make decisions about your
spending that you don't always like. It's tempting to give
in to those wants and forget about what we've said we
really need. We could encounter that old "see it, want it,
gotta have it now" feeling that leads us to impulse spending. If you do spend impulsively, it's important to stop
and reflect on the circumstances. What triggered the behavior? Did satisfying that impulse bring you closer to
your goal of achieving a sense of peace and security? Remember the principle of "do no harm" spending. It will
help curb those impulses.

Figure 5.9 shows Susan's month-end review of her FOOD
category (days 17–30 of the month have been omitted). Notice
that the planned amounts differed from her actual amounts;
she ended up spending more on food than she anticipated. This
was because of reason 1 above: she didn't have a realistic idea
of what food would actually cost. However, she'll be able to use
this new information as she makes future spending plans. To do
your month-end review, simply add up the amounts you spent in

Figure 5.9. Susan's Month-End Review

FOOD	Month Plan	Adjustments	Adjusted Plan	1	2	3	4	5	6	7	8	9
Groceries	400.00		400.00		127.56			15.85				82.64
Meals out — Susan												
Meals out — family	25.00		25.00									
School lunches	20.00		20.00					5.00				
Fast-food takeout	45.00		45.00									
Coffee/tea out	60.00		60.00	3.15	3.15	3.15	3.15	3.15	3.15		3.15	3.15
Snacks for the boys	15.00		15.00				3.25	3.25				
Drive-through runs after sports	35.00		35.00	5.25				5.25				5.25
TOTAL FOOD	600.00		600.00	8.40	130.71	3.15	6.40	32.50	3.15	0	3.15	91.04

FOOD (continued)	10	11	12	13	14	15	16	31	Month Total	Difference
Groceries	5.47						99.82		496.80	(96.80)
Meals out — Susan										
Meals out — family										25.00
School lunches			5.00						20.00	
Fast-food takeout									22.50	22.50
Coffee/tea out	3.15	3.15	3.15	3.15		3.15	3.15	3.15	85.05	(25.05)
Snacks for the boys	3.25						3.25		16.25	(1.25)
Drive-through runs after sports			5.25				5.25		42.00	(7.00)
TOTAL FOOD	11.87	3.15	13.40	3.15	0	3.15	111.47	3.15	682.60	(82.60)

each subcategory, and then each category, to arrive at your totals. Enter the totals in the MONTH TOTAL column, then subtract your MONTH TOTAL in that category or subcategory from the ADJUSTED PLAN amount. A positive number means you stayed within your plan and have some money left over, while a negative number indicates that you spent more than your planned amount.

CONGRATULATIONS! You've just completed the first month of your spending-plan process. This is *huge*! Take a moment to let it sink in that you have begun to cross that bridge from where you have been in your financial life to where you want to be. You have made the first strides in changing old patterns. You're coming out of the financial fog and gaining clarity.

Some shampoo bottles carry the instructions "Lather. Rinse. Repeat." For monthly spending plans, it's "Create. Implement. Repeat." Not only have you created your first monthly spending plan, but you've also created the template for future plans, and now you just repeat the process. Each month this process gets easier and easier. It takes less and less time because you've already developed the system for making your plan. As you see the plan work, you'll also be approaching the planning process with excitement rather than fear, because you'll know the rewards it gives you.

A LIFELONG UPWARD SPIRAL

As you start living with your personal spending plan, you'll begin to see possibilities. First, you'll see the possibility that a life of financial chaos, confusion, and suffering can come to an end. But the absence of chaos is not a fulfilled life; there's much more to be had. As you work your individualized plan, possibilities begin to become realities — a new blossom of hope and imagination will emerge, and your dreams will expand. The most exciting part of improving your relationship with money is not merely that you stop the downward spiral of financial troubles and the force of the Money/Life Drain, but that you begin an upward spiral of financial health, stability, and vitality.

An expansive spending plan is not only about having more money to spend. It's also about having more freedom to do the things that have meaning for you. This could involve purchasing something you've been dreaming about. But an expansive spending plan can involve much more than just saving for big-ticket items. It could mean gaining the freedom to work fewer hours so you can coach your kids' little league team. Or perhaps you dream of taking a sabbatical and traveling for several months. Maybe you've imagined having a large enough income and stable enough finances that you could start a foundation, contribute substantially to a cause you believe in, or change careers to one you'd find more satisfying. This is about more than just having a wish list of stuff you want to buy. It's about imagining the life you want. I think of this expansive experience as the upward spiral of Financial Recovery, which is the opposite of the Money/Life Drain.

The final step in the spending-plan process will help you begin to realize the full potential of the upward spiral.

Step 8: Create an Annual Spending Plan

Now that you've gotten comfortable with creating and implementing monthly spending plans, you're ready to go on to what I call the "graduate school" of spending plans: the annual spending plan. Creating an annual plan helps you expand your view and begin to look at the possibilities you can create for you and your family.

To create your annual spending plan, you'll repeat steps 1 through 7 of creating your monthly spending plan but with slight modifications. Following are some guidelines for the annual-spending-plan process:

- You'll use the categories and subcategories that you created for your monthly plan, including periodic/non-monthly expenses.
- You'll use the same basic materials (trackers, account information, your calendar, etc.), but you'll also need your monthly spending plan(s) on hand.
- For each subcategory, you will enter the amount you think you'll need for the coming year. In many subcategories (but not all), this simply means multiplying your monthly amount by twelve.
- You'll see if your plan works by comparing your estimated annual expenses with your estimated annual income.
- If you need to make adjustments during the course of the year, you can brainstorm ways to spend less or earn more, just as you did for your monthly plan. You'll make adjustments to your plan while still keeping your needs in mind.
- As you go through each month, you'll compare your actual spending to your planned amounts on your annual plan to see if you're still on course.
- At the end of the year, you'll compare your planned spending and income to your actual spending and income. If your planned annual spending differed from your actual spending you'll explore the possible reasons.
- If you're using the MoneyMinder System, the program will keep a running balance of your annual totals as well as your monthly totals.
- As you might expect, the most common time of year to create an annual plan is in December, for the upcoming year. However, some clients choose to create annual

spending plans for the remainder of a current year. For example, if a client started creating monthly plans in March and was comfortable with the process by late June, she might choose to create an annual plan for the remainder of the year, from March through December. This would give her valuable information for planning the second half of the year.

Figure 5.10 shows a portion of Susan's annual spending plan, her FOOD category, on which she has entered her spending totals for January, February, and March. Notice that it contains the same categories and subcategories as does her monthly spending plan. The big difference is that the annual spending plan has columns for months of the year rather than for days of the month. The FULL YEAR TOTAL column reflects all the spending she has done in each subcategory to date, while the REMAINDER column shows how much money she has left to spend in each subcategory for the rest of the year.

If the monthly spending plan is a road map that helps you decide which routes to take, an annual spending plan is a globe that shows you the world of possibilities and helps you seek out where you'd like to go. As you create your annual spending plan, instead of thinking one month ahead, you'll ask yourself, "How much will I need to spend in this subcategory over the course of the next year?" This longer view will prompt you to consider needs that may not be pressing right now. For example, you might not be planning to go to the doctor next month, but you know that in the next year it would be wise to get a checkup or have a medical test such as a mammogram or a cholesterol screening.

Working with an annual plan can be very exciting. Just imagine having a master plan for your life — a plan that looks at the whole year and accounts for all the things you need for the year. It includes your fixed monthly expenses, such as rent or

FIGURE 5.10. SUSAN'S ANNUAL SPENDING PLAN FOR FOOD

FOOD	Year Plan	Adjustments	Adjusted Plan	Jan.	Feb.	March	April	May
Groceries	4800.00			496.80	423.72	469.12		
Meals out — Susan	1200.00			0	55.38	93.20		
Meals out — family	300.00			0	30.50	22.70		
School lunches	180.00			20.00	20.00	20.00		
Fast-food takeout	540.00			22.50	48.00	39.60		
Coffee/tea out	720.00			85.05	75.15	63.10		
Snacks for the boys	180.00			16.25	10.00	14.60		
Drive-through runs after sports	300.00			42.00	35.25	39.75		
TOTAL FOOD	8220.00			682.60	698.00	762.07		

FOOD (continued)	June	July	Aug.	Sept.	Oct.	Nov.	Dec.	Full Year Total	Remainder
Groceries								1389.64	3410.36
Meals out — Susan								148.58	1051.42
Meals out — family								53.20	246.80
School lunches								60.00	120.00
Fast-food takeout								110.10	429.90
Coffee/tea out								223.30	496.70
Snacks for the boys								40.85	139.15
Drive-through runs after sports								117.00	183.00
TOTAL FOOD								2142.67	607.33

mortgage payment, multiplied by twelve. It includes all your variable monthly expenses. It also includes your periodic expenses, such as vacations and holidays.

Looking at their monthly expenses on an annual basis can clarify what's important to people. An expense that we incur daily may seem small. When we look at it in our monthly plan, we start to get the picture of how it is adding up. When we multiply that number by twelve (gulp), it can sometimes be staggering. It might cause us to ask ourselves, "Is this really worth that much money to me?" or "Is this that important to me?" When the answer is "yes," great! You know you're spending money in ways that fit your values and meet your needs. If the answer is "No, I'd really rather use that money another way," that's great too. You now have the knowledge that will allow you to alter your spending choices to align them with what you value. With an annual spending plan, all information is good information.

Also, annual plans operate as "earning plans," not just spending plans. When you design an annual plan and look at all the things you need and desire to spend money on, you see just how much money you really need to make. For example, Susan looked at her annual plan and saw that though she was making it through each month, she would not be able to expand her lifestyle or build for the future unless she earned more money. This prompted her to enroll in the management training program at the bank where she worked. Before long, she was promoted to a managerial position. The higher salary allowed her to create the lifestyle and security she needed.

Many people honestly do not know how much money they need, or want, to make. Working with an annual plan helps people think deeply about their lifestyles and explore what career paths will provide an income that matches their expenses. This is very powerful information. We'll talk a lot more about your relationship with work and earning in chapter 7.

Having a plan in place is also really useful when it comes to managing a big project, such as a kitchen remodel. Many clients have told me that they started a major project like this and ran out of money in the middle. Not only was their project incomplete, but they were left living in a real mess. With an annual plan in place, you'll know before you start a project whether you can manage it, whether you need to delay it, or if it might be wise to take it on in smaller stages.

Of course, the first time people do an annual plan can be quite alarming. Their expenses commonly outweigh their income, as also sometimes happens in monthly plans. But an annual plan is still only a plan — nothing has happened yet. You'll have plenty of time to make adjustments as issues arise.

Just as you did for the monthly spending plan, be sure to flip through your calendar for the upcoming year as you're brainstorming nonmonthly expenses for your annual plans. This can remind you of things such as holidays, birthdays, graduations, and vacations that don't come up monthly. It can also remind you of things like taxes and insurance. If you calculate that your car will need an oil change two to four times a year (depending on your driving habits) and perhaps will need a tune-up once a year, you can put that into your plan, making a reasonable guess as to which month(s) you might take care of these things. Car insurance is sometimes paid quarterly or biannually, so this belongs here too. Home maintenance items such as carpet cleaning or garden supplies may come up seasonally as well.

By using an annual plan, you'll be actually walking across that bridge from the way your financial life has been to the way you want it to be. This is a bridge toward all the possibilities that await you.

A MOMENT OF REFLECTION

Creating a monthly and annual spending plan takes some time and effort. The first month or two are the hardest and require the most time because you're new to the process. It gets easier and takes less time each subsequent month. Once you've created it, learned to maintain it with a few simple steps, and mastered adjusting it to meet your changing needs, your spending plan will take care of you. By investing a comparatively small amount of time, you create a road map for your immediate financial future — and the good feeling that comes from knowing that your finances will be under control as long as you stay on the course you've designed. So ask yourself, "Is my money worth my time?"

In this chapter and the previous one, you've learned about the two most fundamental practices for improving your money situation: tracking and creating a spending plan. By implementing what you've learned, you'll create enormous possibilities for healing your relationship with money.

The biggest benefit of this process is the clarity it brings. With that clarity, the financial fog dissipates. Only then can hope begin to shine through your current situation, no matter how bad it is. This hope will allow you to see as possible the financial life you want for you and your family. Over time, hope becomes confidence, and confidence becomes mastery.

At this point I invite you to pause and reflect. Take time to congratulate yourself for exploring this process. At each stage, every step you take, remember to appreciate yourself for your small and large accomplishments along the way.

CHAPTER SIX

Saving Your Way Out of Debt

Fixing Your Past, Living Your Present,
Securing Your Future

Creditors have better memories than debtors.

— BENJAMIN FRANKLIN

The burden of debt has ruined the lives of millions of people. They're in pain. They're worried. They're feeling hopeless and defeated. Some simply juggle debt — through consolidation loans, second mortgages, loans from family, even bankruptcy. Yet they find the cage of debt once again closing in around them. This time it feels as though there's no way out. Their situations feel desperate.

Debt is often the biggest source of emotional agony for people struggling in their relationship with money. Debt is a burglar that robs us of our quality of life. Debt is an embezzler that silently steals our security for the future. Debt can also commit the ultimate crime: it can kill.

I'm not being figurative here, and I'm not exaggerating. I

mean debt can *literally* kill people. The enormous emotional burden of debt contributes to the progression of stress-related illness. Perhaps most tragic of all, many people feel suicidal because of their debt.

Once while traveling to give a keynote address at a conference about money, I turned on the TV in my hotel room. I was struck by a story of the suicide of a college student. As you can imagine, her mother was in utter despair. After the body of the girl was found, her dorm mate discovered on her bed a splay of maxed-out credit card bills and a suicide note that confessed that shame over debt had caused her to take her life.[1] The grieving mom spoke through tears, wishing her daughter had confided in her about her financial troubles, wishing against all things rational that she could just have her daughter back. I've heard variations on this story too many times.

When people come to me for financial counseling, I can see how hard it is for them to confess how much they owe. I use the word *confess* intentionally, because people have often hidden the amount they owe from the people they love and from themselves. They're ashamed and talk as though they were confessing to a heinous crime. They've often already gone through what they thought were desperate measures. But still, they're stuck.

Debt can trap people of all income levels, all ages, and all cultural backgrounds or political affiliations. We've all read or seen reports of highly paid celebrities, athletes, or politicians who rise to fame and fortune only to crash because of debt.

Many put their lives on hold until that mythical day when they'll be debt-free — but it never comes. Debt dis-ease is cancerous, attacking first our money, then our emotions, then our bodies, then our spirits. But debt dis-ease is treatable and preventable and does not have to pose any further menace. The cure for debt dis-ease requires no scientific funding, no research and development, and no FDA approval. This cure has already been developed and it's simpler than you might think; it's right here in the pages of this chapter.

Of course, there are different kinds of debt, and not all debts are harmful. Certainly when it comes to big-ticket items, such as homes, being able to pay cash is not feasible for most people. These people then operate with a certain amount of debt in the form of mortgages, car loans, student loans, and business loans. But few financial advisers would argue that a sensible mortgage debt is a bad thing. And student loans, although they can be massive, can be a good investment in a promising career. We're focusing in this chapter on a different kind of debt: what some people call consumer debt and what I will refer to simply as credit card debt.

Credit card debt has become an epidemic in the United States, and many people consider it a way of life. Many get their cards with no intention of using them "except for an emergency." But the credit card companies know there will always be some kind of emergency. They seduce us with low starting interest rates, free signing offers of gifts or airline miles, lures of convenience, discounts, and all sorts of other perks. But just like the casinos with their discount buffets and free drinks, the credit industry is set up so that the house always wins.

The house *always* wins.

This is true even if you pay off your cards every month. It's true even if you pay more than minimum payments. It's true if you get free mileage or cash bonus points. It's true if you get free hotel stays or upgrades. The credit card house always wins.

The strategy I teach is about eliminating credit card debt because I want *you* to win, and it can be done.

A REVOLUTIONARY APPROACH
TO STAYING OUT OF DEBT

Believe it or not, to live a financially stable life, the issue is not *getting* out of debt. People get out of debt all the time. Some people are actually quite good at getting out of debt, again and again — the problem is that they just go right back in. As with yo-yo dieting, some find that they have accumulated and paid off debt many times, only to find themselves facing it again. So the real issue is *staying* out of debt.

Understanding your needs and wants, tracking your spending, and building a spending plan form the foundation of Financial Recovery. If you have started tracking and have created a spending plan, you might be starting to see what is possible. But to have true freedom in your life, you'll want to escape the cycle of debt forever — to never fear going back into debt and to have savings for yourself. Yes, these things are possible, and they are far more linked than most people realize.

Many people believe they can't begin saving money until they are free of debt. In fact, saving — even while you're paying down debt — is the key that will free you from the debt cycle forever. I call this "Saving Your Way Out of Debt." This approach to debt and savings sets Financial Recovery apart from other money management programs and makes the process successful for many people who have struggled to get free of debt and stay free.

Once again I ask you to adopt a beginner's mind. My approach to debt and savings may at first seem counterintuitive. I assure you that this approach to debt and savings will yield dramatic changes in your relationship with money and help you make the biggest strides toward a sustainable financial life.

Bookstores, the internet, and money programs are filled with advice and information about debt and savings. It's easy to get overwhelmed and lost in the details. If you want to learn the subtle nuances about credit, interest rates, and improving your credit scores, I recommend consumer advocate Gerri Detweiler's book *The Ultimate Credit Handbook*, which is loaded with detailed, helpful information.

Here in this chapter I offer something you won't find in any other book. It's a simple yet life-changing strategy for getting out of credit card debt, staying out of debt, and simultaneously protecting your future. Perhaps the most transformative aspect of Financial Recovery, Saving Your Way Out of Debt is not just a model; it's a practical system that I and other Financial Recovery counselors have used with real people of all income levels for more than two decades — with great success. Whether you've lived with what seems like a constant debt load for years or you've accumulated and then paid off debt a dozen times, this proven strategy can change your financial life forever. If you currently pay off your credit card balance every month but don't know how you'd possibly begin saving money, this plan is for you too.

Just imagine how it would feel to have *no worries* about debt as part of your life. Imagine also having the security of knowing you had savings to protect you. What choices would you make about where and how you'd spend your money? What kind of lifestyle would you choose? What would you do with your time? How would you feel about your financial future?

I've worked with thousands of people using the strategies I'm going to share with you here. I've seen people who start out as skeptics become believers. I've worked with people who had resigned themselves to a lifetime trapped in a virtual debtors' prison, who then became debt-free and remained so. No, they didn't win the lottery or become the American Idol. They were ordinary people from every income level who made this happen by working with this program.

The first step is to confront your relationship with debt. I encourage you to take some time to complete the following exercise. If debt has been a source of pain for you, isn't it worth figuring out how to have a less painful existence?

Beginning to Understand Your Relationship with Debt

To begin to understand your relationship with debt, respond in detail to the following questions in your money journal.

1. How long has debt been a source of stress, worry, or unhappiness for you? How has this affected your life?
2. Do you feel a sense of shame when you look at your debt balances?
3. Have you ever dug yourself out of debt, swearing you'd never get into it again, but found that you have? How many times?
4. When you look at the balances on your credit cards, do you remember how you spent that money? Or was it for events and purchases from years ago?
5. Have you resorted to any of the following to pay down credit cards: consolidation loans, home equity lines of credit, home refinancing, liquidating investments, tapping into retirement accounts, family loans, borrowing against future inheritance? How has this pattern affected you?
6. Has debt kept you from doing something that is important to you? Describe.
7. Has debt kept you from taking advantage of an opportunity? Describe.
8. Is debt a source of distress for you or others in your family? How so?

OUR INABILITY TO SAVE MONEY

"Save for a rainy day." We've been hearing that since we were kids. But how many of us feel as though it's raining *every* day? It seems impossible to put any money away. We're in financial survival mode, barely making it through each month as it is, much less thinking we have anything *extra* to put aside. Or maybe we have managed to tuck away a little rainy-day money. We promise ourselves we won't touch it, but sooner or later, something happens — the water heater breaks, the car's transmission dies, the kids' tuition bills arrive — and we need to dip into the savings. We watch with discouragement as that balance gets smaller. It was so hard to put it away in the first place. We feel guilty and defeated. After all, we promised ourselves we wouldn't use that money. But there we are, back at square one. That old "Why bother?" feeling crops up again.

For many of us, saving money either feels completely impossible or like a worthless effort, especially if we're struggling with debt too. It feels kind of ridiculous to put money into an account that gets almost nothing in interest, particularly if our credit cards are charging sky-high interest rates.

The feeling that saving is either impossible or futile — or both — is very common. The United States has become a nation of nonsavers. In near-perfect parallel to credit becoming widely available, people stopped saving. We started viewing our credit cards as our emergency funds and rainy-day accounts. (Remember, credit card companies are hoping we see their cards this way.) Many of us started spending all of, or more than, our monthly incomes, living paycheck to paycheck. We're living on the edge. We can't breathe, let alone save any money.

The costs of not having savings are much more than financial, which I learned firsthand many years ago. Long before I started developing Financial Recovery, I was working as a salesperson for a computer company. The company sent me to New England for a six-month training program. This was after a divorce, and with my daughters away at college, I felt very alone in the world. My personal and financial life was in chaos. My credit cards were maxed out. I had nothing in savings. The fact that the company provided housing and a company car was a real blessing. Sadly, a couple of months into my training, my uncle called to tell me that my grandmother had died.

My grandmother had been one of the biggest sources of love and comfort during a childhood that often lacked both. She had continued to be a fountain of affection and wisdom throughout all my life's ups and downs, unconditionally accepting me in whatever condition she found me. I felt stabbed with instant grief and a sense of loss as my uncle talked of her passing and the plans for her funeral. The second stab came when I realized that with no remaining credit and no savings, I had no way to buy a cross-country airline ticket to attend funeral services in California. Looking back, I now know I could have asked my uncle, a friend, or even my ex-husband to buy me a ticket. Any number of people would have helped me. But I had gone to people for financial help before. I felt such shame about being in financial trouble again that I just couldn't bear the thought of asking someone for help.

I missed my grandmother's funeral. To this day, this is something I regret. I would have wanted to honor her, and to be in the comfort of my family. When we lose something that money can buy, we have the chance to make up for it. But the opportunity to experience the celebration of her life and closure that others had at my grandmother's funeral is something I can never get back. My relationship with savings and debt, and my shame about money, denied me this opportunity. I felt robbed of dignity and ravaged by an even deeper level of shame for letting my money troubles force me into this position.

Through savings we can create the flexibility to handle the unexpected events that life dishes out — whether the loss of a loved one or just the everyday expenses that come along.

Our history with savings can sometimes clue us in as to why saving money may be difficult. Do you remember your first experience with saving money? Were you encouraged to save for something you wanted? Did you have a special place to save your money? Or did you struggle to save anything, finding that your money quickly disappeared as soon as you saved it? One of my clients remembers saving money in a piggy bank as a little girl and then having her mother "borrow" the money for groceries, but never pay it back. She remembers thinking, "Why bother? The money just disappears." Other clients have described how they started to invest money but then saw that the fees they were charged were greater than what they made on their investments. Again, a "Why bother?" attitude prevailed.

Most people were not taught anything about saving money. It was a vague concept at best and not something they feel they've ever had great success with. They've inherited conflicting messages. They were told they should save but were not given information about how to save, or for what purpose. What do you remember about the messages you were given about saving money?

EXERCISE

Beginning to Understand Your Relationship with Savings

To begin to understand your relationship with savings, answer the following questions in your money journal.

1. What is your first memory of saving money? What did you use the money for?
2. Do you currently have a savings account? If so, what are you saving for?

3. Does having a savings account sometimes feel like an impossible goal? Why?
4. If you don't have any savings right now, how does that make you feel?
5. Have you ever had a savings account and then felt guilty when you needed to use the money?
6. Have you used savings to pay down debt, then accumulated the debt all over again?
7. Do you find that you use savings for other expenses than you intended it for? If so, describe your experiences.
8. Has a lack of savings ever kept you from doing something that was important to you? What was it?
9. Has a lack of savings ever kept you from being able to take advantage of an opportunity? What was it?

Reflect on your responses. Write about your experience with saving money: your feelings about it, what worked, what didn't. What overall thoughts emerge as you think about saving money?

YOUR REFLECTIONS in the two exercises in this chapter might not only reveal your relationship with and beliefs about debt and savings but also uncover some common misconceptions you hold as well. The very first thing we have to change about savings is how we think about it. As long as we see savings as impossible, vague of purpose, or worthless, it will never be a viable tool. I know, you may have tried before. I know, it's discouraging. I felt exactly the same way. But in Financial Recovery I teach a different savings mind-set, a hierarchical saving strategy. When people start to experience the success of this strategy, they become believers.

THE "SAVING YOUR WAY OUT OF DEBT" RATIONALE

When I start to introduce the Saving Your Way Out of Debt approach to clients and at conferences, people often respond with

blank stares and furrowed brows. My audience sometimes includes accountants and other money professionals, people who
understand numbers. "But shouldn't you pay down high-interest
debt before starting low-interest saving?" they ask.

This perfectly logical, mathematically accurate thinking is
what keeps people caught in a cycle of debt. In reality, we usually spend our way into debt, so we have to save our way out of
debt.

Remember, Financial Recovery is not just a program about
numbers or an exercise in math. This is about your relationship
with money too. For now, let's look beyond the math at why debt
and savings must be inextricably linked for this process to work
emotionally as well as mathematically.

My client Emily was a young chiropractor. Like my accountant friends, she assumed that saving would come later, after
she'd paid down her debt. But she learned that by saving her way
out of debt, she could build a life of financial stability instead of
yo-yo debting. We'll follow Emily's story throughout this chapter
to learn about the successful strategy of Saving Your Way Out of
Debt.

CASE STUDY
Emily, Part 1

Emily spent her first four years out of chiropractic school
working in a group practice in Los Angeles. But she'd always
dreamed of opening her own office in the San Francisco Bay
Area, where her family lived. It took a lot to relocate and start
her practice there. Between business expenses, malpractice
insurance, and living expenses, Emily found that her income
didn't always stretch as far as she would have liked. On top

of this, she had gut-busting payments on her student loans. It felt as if she'd never be able to pay them off.

Through college and chiropractic school, and then the long hours of establishing a new practice, Emily had worked hard for a very long time. In her limited free time she felt as though she deserved a little pampering, whether it was through shopping with her friends or enjoying San Francisco's fine dining.

Emily had a part-time receptionist but didn't feel she could afford a bookkeeper too, so she did the insurance billing herself on the weekends. Because she had a hard time keeping up with the insurance billings, there was sometimes quite a lag before these checks came. During gaps between payments, Emily relied on credit cards to make up the shortfall. As the balances rose, she felt increasingly worried.

When reimbursement checks arrived, Emily promptly paid her credit card balances down to zero. Instantly, she felt relief. Each time, she swore that she'd not run up her cards again, but once the relief of paying them off had faded and regular life resumed, she found herself repeating the cycle.

Even when Emily exercised great restraint on optional expenses, something always seemed to happen. One month her car needed new tires. Another, her best friend asked her to be her maid of honor, so Emily used her credit cards to buy her bridesmaid's dress.

In addition to feeling stressed, Emily was embarrassed. "In college I graduated summa cum laude," she said, "but when it comes to money, I just don't seem to be able to figure things out."

Emily kept telling herself that she'd start a savings account with the next insurance check. She wanted the comfort of a financial cushion. But when each check arrived, it simply didn't make sense to her to get low interest in a savings account while she was paying high interest to creditors.

When people are struggling with debt, they often make the same choice Emily did. They assume they should throw all their available money at their debt. It feels silly to them to put money in a savings account that earns almost nothing in interest when paying 20 to 30 percent in interest on credit cards.

Although this line of thinking sounds mathematically logical, there's a big problem with it. *It is very short-term thinking.* It works to pay off your debt with all your available money only if you assume that tomorrow the world ends. Well, okay, to be less dramatic — it works to throw all your available money at your debt only if you assume that nothing out of the ordinary will ever happen again. But the one thing you can be sure of is that "life happens." Surprise expenses will always crop up, no matter how thoroughly you plan. Many people pay for these surprises with credit cards, and using their cards while trying to pay down their debt leaves them very frustrated.

Before we explore the steps involved in Saving Your Way Out of Debt, I want you to fully grasp how the debt cycle works. Assume for a moment that you get the lovely surprise of a tax refund. You use the whole thing to pay down a whopper of a credit card bill. *Whew! That's a relief.* You vow that you'll pay your card in full every month from now on and that you'll start putting money into savings. Now, envision something happening — your water heater springs a leak, or you need to take your cat to the vet, or your kids need back-to-school clothes. Remember those periodic expenses we talked about in the previous chapter — all those nonmonthly, irregular expenses that always seem to surprise us? Good surprises, bad surprises, everyday expenses — they all cost money. Where will the money come from to pay for these things? You used all your available money to pay down your debt. There sits that credit card with a big fat zero balance. It has begun to seem like your personal emergency savings account. Almost certainly, you'll end up having to charge these expenses. Once this happens, it's easy to feel as though you've blown it and slip into "oh well" thinking. The familiar pattern of charging starts all over again and the debt cycle resumes.

Not having savings is a major reason people get into debt — even when they don't have problems controlling their spending. The cycle is vicious! Are you ready to exit the cycle?

THE DEBT PYRAMID

The ultimate goal is to eliminate debt entirely, but most people can't achieve this goal in one step. Instead, they need to work toward it systematically. Inspired again by Maslow's Hierarchy of Needs, I view the journey out of debt in a hierarchy as well (see figure 6.1).

There are a hundred programs out there for reducing and eliminating debt. If you've ever had a sleepless night and tuned in to late-night TV, you've likely seen somebody selling a system for managing debt. They know their audience — worries about debt often keep people awake. There are three big flaws in most debt-reduction programs.

- They skip level one — debt stabilization — starting prematurely on reducing debt before debt has been stabilized.

- They don't address savings at all, so when "life happens," a credit card is the only option.   .
- They don't take emotional factors, needs, and feelings of deprivation into account.

These approaches might help you get out of debt in the short term, but they offer nothing for staying out of debt. Financial Recovery is different. So let's get started with level 1 — it's time to stabilize!

FIGURE 6.1. THE DEBT PYRAMID

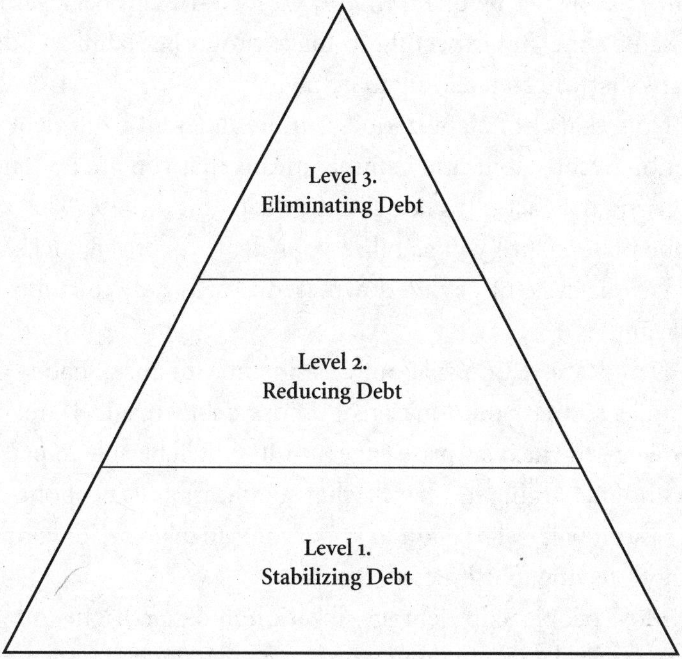

Level 3.
Eliminating Debt

Level 2.
Reducing Debt

Level 1.
Stabilizing Debt

DEBT PYRAMID, LEVEL 1: STABILIZING DEBT

The bottom level of the debt pyramid, and the first step to freeing yourself from the debt cycle, is debt stabilization. This step is at the base of the pyramid, just as basic survival was at the base of

Maslow's Hierarchy of Needs. As the foundation for eventually living completely debt-free, it is the biggest part of the pyramid. It's also the hardest step to take because it requires you to shift your thinking about your relationship with debt.

Getting and staying out of debt requires a fundamental psychological and emotional shift. If you're driving down the highway at sixty-five miles an hour and you need to back up, you can't just jam the car into reverse. You first have to bring your vehicle to a stop. Similarly, you cannot simultaneously use credit cards as part of your monthly money management while stabilizing your debt. That would be like trying to go forward and backward at the same time and expecting to make progress. Stabilizing debt means that you stop adding to it.

Note that debt stabilization is quite different from debt reduction. Debt stabilization simply means that you are no longer incurring new debt. It's not about getting out of debt. That will happen later. Until you stabilize your debt, you'll stay locked in the vicious cycle of paying down credit cards only to run them up again.

Debt stabilization is about creating new financial habits and attitudes so that you don't create more debt. Imagine knowing that when the next surprise expense hits, you'll be able to pay for it without charging it. That is what stabilization is all about. Believe me, it will feel so good to know you can take care of yourself without having to use a credit card.

Most people skip debt stabilization and start right into reducing their debt — in other words, paying it down. I understand this desire: debt feels awful and we want it gone. Emily was doing this. She wanted her debt gone, but she was trying to reduce her debt while simultaneously adding more debt to it. Starting prematurely with paying down your debt while you're still either using your credit cards or in danger of using them if something happens keeps you stuck in the debt cycle for decades. This is like sitting in a boat with a grapefruit-sized hole in the side and bailing out the gushing water with a thimble. You can never get ahead of the leak. Similarly, you simply cannot get out of debt if you are still incurring new debt. Surprise expenses will crop up. They always do.

I know this may be hard, and I know that the thought of not using credit cards can bring up fear or make you feel over-whelmed. It may mean that you have to temporarily get very, very creative at meeting your needs if you can't resort to doing so with your charge card. But you can do this. This is why we covered spending plans and ways to meet your needs before tackling debt. If you've built a monthly spending plan as we discussed in chap-ter 5, you have the tool you need to live within your means *with-out* charging any of your bills or expenses. For now, I'm going to ask you, once again, to trust the process.

You may be thinking, "But I *am* stabilizing my debt. I'm pay-ing more than the minimum payments." This is great, but if you're continuing to use your cards while you're paying them down, you're still trying to bail out water while more rushes through the hole. And it will take you a lot longer to get out of debt if you do it this way. Even if you manage to get ahead of the water and bail out more than is coming through the hole, you can never, ever rest. The hole will always let in more water. Tired yet? Don't stop bailing the water!

You must plug the hole first. You simply must stop using your credit cards if you want your debt to never grow again — or to stop going up and down and up and down and up…

Remember, in your spending plan you've created a category for debt repayment. You may be able to make only minimum payments, and this is fine for now. As long as you are paying at least minimum payments on every debt, regularly and on time, and not charging anything further, you're stabilizing debt. Is this ideal? No, of course not. Is this alone going to get you out of debt? No. But this is where to start. This is about bringing that racing debt car to a stop. As you read the rest of this chapter, you'll see how you can put your debt into reverse.

THE SAVINGS PYRAMID

You may have been thinking that the next step after *stabilizing debt* is to move up the Debt Pyramid to reducing and then eliminating debt. Instead, this is the point when we must link debt to savings. It is important to understand that these two seemingly separate things actually go hand in hand. Not having savings is a major reason people get into debt. You spent your way into debt; now you must save your way out of it. By creating periodic savings after you've stabilized your debt, you can climb out of the black hole of chronic debting.

Figure 6.2 shows what I call the savings pyramid. As with the debt pyramid, the bottom level — periodic savings — will form the firm foundation of your relationship with savings and is one of the keys to saving your way out of debt.

We tend to think of our savings as something we should never touch. If we do touch it, it means that we've blown it, and we feel guilty and defeated. But there are different kinds of savings for different intentions in your life. As the pyramid depicts, there are three different levels of savings. Periodic savings is at the base (level 1). This money is for periodic, nonmonthly expenses. Safety-net savings is next (level 2). This money is meant to be used if you have an interruption in income. Long-term investments (level 3) make up the third type of savings. We'll explore each of these levels in more detail below.

FIGURE 6.2. THE SAVINGS PYRAMID

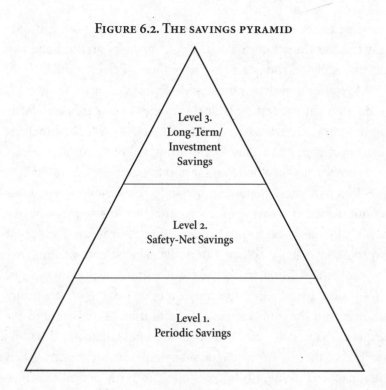

Level 3.
Long-Term/
Investment
Savings

Level 2.
Safety-Net Savings

Level 1.
Periodic Savings

SAVINGS PYRAMID, LEVEL 1: PERIODIC SAVINGS

Periodic savings, the most important type of savings when you want to stabilize and break free from the debt cycle, is one of the keys to making your entire financial life work. Without periodic savings, your financial situation is a house of cards. Even if you have investment savings or equity in your house, without periodic savings your other assets are at risk.

Simply put, periodic savings is money you set aside to help cover your periodic expenses. You build a certain amount into your personal spending plan each month and deposit that money into a simple savings account (not an investment account — you need to be able to access this money). Then when a periodic

expense arises, such as a car repair or a family vacation, you simply transfer the money back into your primary account and pay
for the expense. You don't have to put it on a credit card!

Keep in mind that your periodic savings is meant to be used,
guilt-free. You are setting aside this money to care for periodic or
nonmonthly expenses (car registrations, taxes, membership dues,
etc.) rather than charging them. Being without periodic savings
is a sure way to keep on charging and to never get free of debt.

Every month I deposit money into my periodic savings account, which is a savings account attached to my checking account. It feels good to put money into it, but it also feels good
to sometimes use it. When a periodic expense comes along, expected or not, I first try to pay for it without using my savings.
Every time I have a nonmonthly expense, I don't automatically
transfer money from savings. We're all used to absorbing these
expenses as best we can. The trouble comes when you can't absorb all of them — or when too many expenses hit at once. When
that happens to me, I transfer money from my periodic savings
account so I don't have to put anything on a credit card.

Of course, at the beginning of some months I know I'm going
to use some of my periodic savings to help me. When I went on a
big trip last year, I planned on using some of my periodic savings.

That's right, periodic expenses aren't always unfortunate
ones — we love some of them. Who doesn't like vacations? We
just don't like their debt aftermath. But when the vacation is paid
for with funds we've set aside in advance, we can discover a whole
new level of R&R while we're away.

In your spending plan you created categories for anticipated
nonmonthly expenses. Those need to be paid from somewhere,
right? Your monthly plan may cover some, or all, of these. But those
whose spending plans are tight tend to pay for these nonmonthly
expenses by, you guessed it, charging them. Remember that I had

you create a category in your spending plan called PERIODIC SAVINGS? When you have a periodic expense that you can't cover, you can transfer money from this savings account into your primary account and pay for the expense; you won't have to put it on a credit card. Having this savings will stabilize not only your financial life but your worry and stress level too.

I know this may sound impossible. How do you save if your monthly plan is already tight? Even on tight plans, saving must be a priority. Without savings, these periodic expenses (expected or not) cannot be covered without accruing more debt — or otherwise "destabilizing" your debt. Then the cycle continues and nothing changes.

Debt stabilization (the first level of the debt pyramid) is dependent on periodic savings (the first level of the savings pyramid); that is, the only way to keep debt stabilized — to not add to your debt — is to have a way to pay for periodic expenses when they occur. The process of getting out of debt, and staying out, is inextricably linked to the process of saving. Once you have implemented these two basic and essential parts of these pyramids, you are free to move farther up the hierarchy toward financial freedom (see figure 6.3).

Funding Your Periodic Savings Account

You may be wondering where you're supposed to find the money to deposit into your periodic savings every month, and the answer might seem counterintuitive. One place to look is your monthly expenses, including debt payments. If you are paying more than minimums on your credit card bills but saving nothing, then you are setting yourself up for inevitable problems down the road. So for a time it might be necessary to reduce your credit card payments to minimums only and put the extra money into periodic savings. For example, if you regularly pay $1,000 in debt

FIGURE 6.3. THE LINK BETWEEN DEBT AND SAVINGS

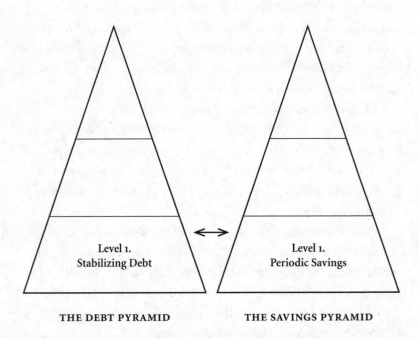

Level 1.
Stabilizing Debt

Level 1.
Periodic Savings

THE DEBT PYRAMID   **THE SAVINGS PYRAMID**

Debt and savings are inextricably linked. You must stabilize your debt and establish periodic savings before you can move up to higher levels of the pyramids.

payments but your minimum payments add up to $750, consider
paying only $750 a month and putting the remaining $250 into
your monthly periodic savings account.

If you pay the $1,000 and your car breaks down next month,
how will you avoid putting the repairs on a credit card? It is better
to make minimum payments for a while and focus on stabilizing your debt. Otherwise, you will likely be very frustrated when
something does happen and you're forced to pull out that credit
card. (Of course, if you can build a little extra into your debt
repayment plan without going into deprivation mode and while
still making a periodic savings contribution, by all means, do it.)

Accountants and math experts among you might be calculating. Of course, interest on credit accounts will be higher than the interest you're earning through any savings accounts. Mathematically, that's true. But we're dealing with more than math here. We're creating a way for you to break the debt cycle and keep your debt stable while still living your life and meeting your emotional, financial, and spiritual needs. Besides, even if you're currently paying more than minimum payments, you've probably been paying interest for years. Making minimum payments for a short while longer in order to move toward reducing and eliminating debt *forever* will end up paying for itself a thousand times during the course of your future financial life. By creating periodic savings, you can climb out of the deep hole of debting and keep from falling back in.

If you want to stop debting, you have to start saving.

CASE STUDY
Emily, Part 2

After Emily began working the Financial Recovery process, the first thing she did to stop the debt cycle was to stop charging. She tucked her credit cards into a safe place and switched to a cash system — that is, she paid for everything with the money she had. She used her debit card, wrote checks, and often paid her bills online out of her checking account. She did not use a credit card. She spent only the money she had in her account. She continued to track all her spending. Emily recognized that her impulse buys were automatically reduced because spending her actual money (not using borrowed money) and tracking made her more conscious of and connected to her money. By converting to a cash-only system and building a reasonable spending plan that took care of her needs along the way, Emily stabilized her debt.

Into Emily's monthly spending plan we built minimum payments on her existing credit card balances and her student loan. At first it was hard for her to resist paying more, but she trusted the process of Financial Recovery and decided to give it a try.

When her next insurance check arrived, rather than completely paying off her credit card debt, Emily created a savings account that was designated for periodic, nonmonthly expenses. A couple of months later when she hosted her friend's bridal shower, she was able to pay for it guilt-free and in cash — without touching her credit card. She continued this pattern of transferring a portion of each insurance check into savings until she felt prepared for nonmonthly expenses such as her car repairs and other unanticipated expenses. Because she was self-employed, she had to plan for quarterly taxes and insurance too. She also earmarked part of her savings for a getaway weekend she and her girlfriends wanted to take six months later.

Having a savings account to use for periodic expenses, combined with stabilizing her debt (not continuing to charge on her card), built a firm foundation for Emily's future saving and debt reduction. It freed her from the debt cycle and provided her with peace of mind.

Once you have your debt stabilized and are funding your periodic savings, you can look at starting to reduce your debt.

DEBT PYRAMID, LEVEL 2: REDUCING DEBT

Please note that if you try to start with debt reduction while you're still using credit cards, it's going to be nearly impossible. Stabilizing debt must precede reducing debt.

Once your debt is stabilized (you're no longer incurring new debt), you're saving monthly for your periodic expenses, and you've got a livable spending plan, you can move up the debt pyramid to the second level to start reducing your debt. But first, I encourage you to take what I call a Fearless Financial Inventory.

EXERCISE

Your Fearless Financial Inventory

In this exercise, you'll take another step toward "radical financial clarity" by finding out and listing exactly what you owe and what you own — the balances of your checking account, savings account (if you have one), credit cards, loans, and investment accounts as well as your valuable possessions. To get started, create a new spreadsheet or get out your money journal, and add the title MY FEARLESS FINANCIAL INVENTORY.

Below the title, add the heading WHAT I OWN, then begin by listing the balances of your checking and savings accounts. Below those balances, list the balances of any investment or retirement accounts, home equity, and the approximate worth of any other valuable assets, such as artwork or jewelry, that you might have.

Next, add a second heading: WHAT I OWE. Look at your spending and income plan. Your debt repayment category should include all the credit card accounts and loans you make payments on, so you can either copy and paste each subcategory (Master-Card, Sears card, student loan, and so on) into your spreadsheet or write it down. Don't leave out any loans you may have received from family members or friends, even if you haven't started repaying them. Also include your mortgage balance and car payment, if you have them. Next to each debt you'll write the total amount you owe (you can find this amount on your monthly statement or by logging into your online account). For each credit card or loan, also write the interest rate.

Once you've listed all your debts, pause and take a few breaths. Some people find it discouraging to see their meager account balances and all their debt balances staring them in the face, but remind yourself of the "fearless" part of this inventory — by becoming fully conscious of your balances, you are taking a very courageous step. You are asserting that you will no longer be in denial or financial fog. And I assure you that this awareness will help you toward freeing yourself from the shackles of debt. Also, remind yourself of all the nonfinancial assets you have, such as relationships with loved ones, spiritual practices, or fulfilling hobbies or skills, which are priceless.

Now THAT YOU HAVE A CLEAR PICTURE of your financial landscape, you can use your spending plan to determine the amount that you are going to pay toward reducing your debt each month. Once you decide on this amount, then you can "power pay."

"Power paying" is a commonly advocated method that tells you to pay your cards off in order of interest rates. Specifically, here is how to do this: List your credit cards and their interest rates. The credit card with the highest interest rate (not the highest balance) is the one you "target." You pay this card's minimum payment, plus any extra money. Then you make a minimum payment on all the other cards.

When the highest-interest card is paid off, you then "roll over" all the money you had been paying on this card to the card with the next-highest interest rate. All the other cards still get minimum payments only. As you continue to pay off each card, roll over the payment for that card onto the payment for the next card. Continue to do this until all your debt is gone.

For the most part, I agree with this method (assuming some-one has first stabilized his debt), but I would add one caveat. It is often psychologically easier to approach this phase of your recovery if you target the card with the lowest balance first. I want you to have a sense of accomplishment! If you have a balance of $7,000 on one card and $500 on another, it can be very frustrating to target the $7,000 card first, even if it has the higher interest rate. You'll still be paying on both cards for a long time. I would suggest that you target the $500 card. Pay only the minimum on the $7,000 card and target any extra debt payment funds toward the $500. You will feel great when it is gone and you can turn your attention to the larger debt. This method is often called "snowballing."

The big revelation here is that you can begin to feel more financially secure before you've eliminated debt. I think of this as *living free from debt even before you are debt-free*. Because you are tracking and you have a spending plan, you're not frittering away money unconsciously. This is the payoff.

Reducing debt, particularly if it is large to start with, will take some time. While it may not be speedy, this system is true, pre-dictable, and effective. As you are reducing your debt you can't just put your life on hold. Life is to be lived. That's why your spending plan should include taking care of your needs even while you're paying down debt.

What's important here is that you *are* paying down debt, not accumulating more debt, and doing it within a livable spending plan. This state of affairs is sustainable for however long it takes you to eliminate your debt. Again, this is how you can actually be living free from debt even while you are not yet debt-free.

Of course, the higher your debt, the slower the process of

debt reduction will be. But please, reassure yourself: going slowly in the right direction is enormously better than going in the wrong direction at any speed.

Speeding Up the Process by Adjusting Your Spending Plan

Seeing those debt balances go down — even if it happens slowly — can be very motivating. Some people itch to reduce their debt more quickly. There's nothing wrong with that as long as you don't make your spending plan so tight that you end up charging, can't continue contributing to your periodic savings, or are going into deprivation mode. As Emily's debt started to disappear, she found creative ways to do away with it even faster.

CASE STUDY
Emily, Part 3

Emily's goal was to be free of credit card debt. She wanted to permanently end the debt cycle that she had found herself trapped in. To do this, she had to go hunting in her spending plan for areas in which there might be flexibility she hadn't noticed before. She got creative.

Because she lived near her office, Emily rarely used her car. She chose to trade it in for a less expensive used car. This eliminated her car payment and reduced her insurance premium. She then took the amount of her former car payment and the difference in her insurance costs and applied them directly to her debt repayment. She was more than willing to make this change to help eliminate this big stressor from her life as quickly as possible. She watched her credit card balances go down even faster, and her spending plan still worked. Emily did not feel deprived at all.

You'll be surprised how flexible your spending plan can get when it's designed to meet your needs. Some things that once seemed essential can begin to appear optional because you have bigger goals in mind.

SAVINGS PYRAMID, LEVEL 2: SAFETY-NET SAVINGS

When you look at the second level of the savings pyramid, you'll see "Safety-Net Savings." If the U.S. economic crisis of 2008 and beyond taught us nothing else, it's that everybody needs a safety net. Many people lost their jobs. Self-employed people saw drastic reductions in business and loss of income. Whether you are self-employed or work for someone else, it's really important to have a plan for the possibility of a reduction in or loss of income. A safety-net savings account is designed to cover your living expenses if your income is interrupted *for any reason*. This is separate from your periodic savings account: your periodic savings account is meant to be used for periodic expenses; your safety net is to be used only if you have an interruption in income.

Everybody needs safety-net savings. The exact amount will depend on the nature of the work you do, your income, and how vulnerable to interruption it is. As with the periodic savings account, you can start small. The idea of trying to save three to six months of income seems impossible for most of us, so most people don't even try. I advise people to start small. Begin by trying to accumulate enough to cover groceries for a month. You'll build this over time, and soon you'll have enough to cover a month's rent or mortgage payment. When you commit to the act of building your safety-net savings and then follow through by depositing into it every month, the savings will eventually add up to be enough to bridge the gap if your income is disrupted. Of course, once you're no longer paying down debt, the amount you were paying toward your credit card bills can roll right into savings without changing your monthly spending plan one bit. At that point, you can build your safety net much more quickly.

Many people view disability insurance as their safety net. If your employer provides this, that's terrific (as long as you remain employed). As a result, you may need less in your safety-net account than some other people do. However, for many, particularly those who are self-employed, disability insurance can be prohibitively expensive or not available at all. Whether it's because of your health history, because you're in a dangerous profession, or for some other reason, you may be insurance ineligible. That makes safety-net savings even more crucial.

Even if you can get disability insurance, you can still benefit, starting today, from a safety-net account. If you're paying for disability insurance, you could pay significantly less in premiums if you have a few months of your income protected in your safety-net account. A policy that kicks in after three or six months of disability is *by far* less expensive than one that starts right away.

Acrobats on the high trapeze always have a safety net below. Of course, this is in case of the horrible event of a fall. But the net is for more than that. The presence of the net offers the acrobats the confidence and freedom to really fly. Similarly, safety-net savings does more than just protect us from the possibility of employment disaster or health crisis. It also offers us the freedom to create new possibilities and to soar in our careers. That's why I think of this account as a "freedom fund."

If you have dreams beyond the current job you hold, a freedom fund can create the possibility to think beyond what you're doing. Perhaps you eventually want to take a break from your current job to get some more education. Maybe you want to start your own business, relocate, or take a sabbatical. You'd like to write a novel, volunteer for Habitat for Humanity, or join a mountain-climbing expedition. Your freedom fund is to be used for whenever there is an interruption of income, for whatever reason — even if that reason is voluntary.

Of course, leaving any job must be a well-thought-out decision, particularly in times of high unemployment. But with safety-net savings, you are free to imagine and create other possibilities. You don't have to be locked in job prison. Even if you don't choose to leave your job, knowing that you could if you needed to can be very liberating. No one likes feeling stuck. Having safety-net savings can eliminate that feeling.

DEBT PYRAMID, LEVEL 3: ELIMINATING DEBT

If you stick to this plan, the day will come when your debt is eliminated. When you imagined being debt-free, it might have seemed like only a fantasy. I have celebrated this fantasy becoming reality hundreds of times with people who have used the Saving Your Way Out of Debt plan. People who felt imprisoned for decades freed themselves by using this simple method of eliminating debt. Clients have literally danced in my office when they finally paid off the last of their debt. I've danced with them too! But let me remind you that your Financial Recovery journey should include many celebrations along the way. Celebrate when you get your debt stabilized. Cheer when you pay off one credit card or that loan from your parents that they never thought you would repay. Applaud yourself when you make deposits into your periodic savings account, and clap even harder when you use that account to pay for an unexpected expense without using your credit card.

Don't Get Pulled Back into the Trap

As satisfying as it is, there's one big problem with being free of debt. Those zero balances on credit cards sometimes behave like ghosts, haunting us, calling us. It can be so tempting to rationalize an impulsive out-of-plan purchase by saying, "Hey, it's okay. I don't have any other debt." People start to see all that available credit as money that's available for use. The credit card spiderweb entices them with its shimmering strands of free airline miles and instant cash. But the black widow of debt awaits them in that web.

Reward programs have become the ultimate lure for credit card companies. Many people accelerate their debt problems by using their credit cards for everything from groceries to drive-through fast food. They do this thinking, "I was going to spend it anyway. I might as well get a free trip out of it."

This kind of logic goes sour when you do the math. Ahem, accountants, we might need your skills here. Let's tabulate the costs of rewards programs.

- When you use credit you typically spend more because you're less conscious of your spending.
- Many credit cards that offer rewards also have annual fees.
- If you're not paying your balance in full every month, you're paying interest.
- Excessive credit usage often taps into money you'd otherwise use for more satisfying spending that meets your real needs.
- If you actually accrue enough bonus miles for you and your family to enjoy a so-called free trip, you'll probably use that same credit card during the trip to overspend again.

When you add up all the negatives, a seemingly free trip ends up costing you a bundle. If you build travel into your spending plan, and use periodic savings to pay for it, the same trip can be purchased for a fraction of the cost. The idea of coming home from a trip knowing that you will have to open a shocking credit card statement a couple of weeks later can ruin a great vacation.

Can airline miles and other reward programs ever really be

free? Sure. If you travel with your company on business and you get to use reward miles for a personal trip; that's a free trip. Otherwise, this is major credit card quicksand.

Don't let those big zeroes on your credit accounts or the lure of "free" stuff seduce you back into credit card debt. It's better to avoid the sticky web of credit cards and remain free of debt forever.

Using your periodic savings to keep you from relying on credit cards to pay for nonmonthly expenses is the best tool you have for remaining free of debt. Just remember not to put this tool away simply because you got out of debt. The goal is to stay that way.

SAVINGS PYRAMID, LEVEL 3: LONG-TERM/INVESTMENT SAVINGS

Long-Term/Investment Savings is at the top of the Savings Pyramid, supported by the other kinds of savings. In placing it at the top, I'm not suggesting that saving for retirement isn't important. It is. It's just that if your *only* savings is in the form of long-term investments and retirement accounts, it almost necessarily shoves you into a debt cycle to function in the present. With debt either eliminated or on the way to elimination, a periodic savings account to keep it stable, and a safety-net account to protect income, long-term investment savings becomes possible, sensible, and much more secure.

> Chains of habit are too light to be felt until they are too heavy to be broken.
> — WARREN BUFFETT

Many people have significant retirement accounts but no habits with regard to monthly periodic savings. Inevitably, enough periodic expenses occur that they have to tap these long-term investments for reasons other than what they were intended for. Tragically, when people have to cash out their IRAs or 401(k)s because of debt or loss of income, the taxes and penalties can be enormous. Worse yet, people often feel so much regret at having to dig into their future savings for their present expenses that their self-esteem takes a hit along with their assets. Remember our discussion of needs. Unmet needs (including feelings of discouragement and low self-esteem) often drive us to spend in self-destructive ways.

I worked with a fellow in his late fifties who had nearly a million dollars in his retirement funds. Wow, that sounds great, doesn't it? But when we looked at his entire financial picture, he was going in the hole every month and using credit cards for regular expenses.

> *Doing more of what doesn't work won't make it work any better.*
> — CHARLES GIVENS

He had $200,000 in credit card debt. He was considering pulling money from his retirement account, even with the huge tax consequences, to pay for the debt. But unless he changed his spending patterns and developed periodic savings, it would be only a matter of time before his cards were charged up again. The seeming security of his future wasn't actually so secure.

Many people think of long-term or investment savings as only for retirement accounts such as their 401(k) plans or IRAs. Retirement savings should be a priority, of course. With people living long lives and expenses always going up, retirement planning is vital to a healthy long-range financial future. A good, ethical investment planner or financial adviser can help you determine the best strategies and the right accounts for investing safely in your future, whether for retirement or for other kinds of long-term investments.

However, long-term savings accounts can also be a place to save for a down payment on a home, college funds for the kids, or some other long-term dream. When you are living in a financially stable way, you are free to look more expansively at the future. Eliminating ongoing credit card debt frees you not only to secure your retirement but also to take advantage of investment opportunities. Whether your expanded life plan includes travel, working less, or the freedom to contribute to causes you hold dear, freeing yourself from debt is a huge part of making that happen.

CASE STUDY
Melanie, Revisited

Remember Melanie, the successful real estate agent from chapter 2? She and her family lived on credit cards between commission checks. Though her income was high, she never felt secure and was stuck in the Money/Life Drain, yo-yoing between paying down debt and then accruing it again. By working the Saving Your Way Out of Debt steps in much the same way that Emily did, Melanie was able to first stabilize her debt, then reduce and eliminate it by building periodic savings and safety-net savings. She used her spending plan to determine how much money she and her family would need if sales dipped drastically and they had to live for up to a year without a commission. She put this into an interest-bearing account that was still liquid enough that she could tap into it without penalty.

Melanie contributed to her IRA accounts and also earmarked some money for real estate investments. She had kicked herself in previous down markets for not having the cash to invest. When the real estate bubble burst and prices plummeted, Melanie was secure. She had a safety net that allowed her to live comfortably without using credit to bridge the gap. What's more, her investment savings allowed her to take advantage of the depressed market and buy an income property. As a skilled and successful real estate agent, she knew how to do this conservatively and with minimum risk.

I've seen this time and time again in my practice. By saving their way out of debt, people can take advantage of opportunities they'd otherwise have missed.

FREEDOM FROM THE INTERNAL DEBTORS' PRISON

In 1833 the United States abolished the use of federal laws that imprisoned people for unpaid debt. Except in regard to unpaid child support and tax obligations, having debt is no longer considered a criminal offense. While people can still go to prison for financial fraud (though not as often as some people might wish they did), there are no longer debtors' prisons in the United States.

Nonetheless, debt can serve as an emotional and psychological prison and even a form of self-punishment. While very few people are truly masochistic, when it comes to debt, many of us have a way of inflicting and reinflicting punishment on ourselves. Whether it stems from a background of deprivation, deep feelings of shame and guilt, or very low self-esteem, some of us choose debt as our instrument of self-torture.

> *I learned there are troubles of more than one kind. Some come from ahead, others come from behind. But I've bought a big bat. I'm all ready, you see. Now my troubles are going to have trouble with me.*
> — DR. SEUSS

Financial Recovery is a way out. This program can serve to abolish your internal experience of debtors' prison, just as the federal government abolished it nearly two centuries ago. By leveraging the power of savings, you can free yourself from debt. Free from debt and secured by savings, you can experience comfort and peace of mind. You'll know that both your present and your future are protected. I know I'm a freer person today than I was when debt had its stranglehold on me. I know that thousands of people who have put this program into practice share the freedom of this life without the cage of debt and the stone walls of worry.

CHAPTER SEVEN

Your Relationship with Work and Earning

Is Your Work Working for You?

> *Success is not the key to happiness.*
> *Happiness is the key to success.*
> *If you love what you are doing, you will be successful.*

— BUDDHA

For most of us, our work and our money are inseparable. Many people view work as just a means of earning money, but work can be so much more than that. It can be where we express what's important to us, where we utilize our talents and the individual qualities that make us unique. At work we can learn and stretch ourselves in new ways. Our work can be an aspect of our lives where we derive satisfaction, confidence, success, and self-worth. When our work "works" for us, it fulfills many of our needs. When our relationship with work (and the money it provides) is not working, it can be a source of great stress, worry, and unhappiness.

Over the years I've met and worked with many people struggling with work and earning issues: A one-time Grammy winner who'd blown her fortune and was trying to make it on the salary she earned waiting tables part-time. A woman who'd grown up with enormous wealth, now living from inheritance to inheritance, unable to imagine how she might support herself if the money dried up. An investment broker who was constantly living for his next "big deal" but earned nothing in the years between his big payoffs. A contractor whose business seemed to eat money faster than he could make it. An administrative assistant who felt stuck because she didn't think she could ever earn any more money. The list goes on and on.

These people don't necessarily struggle in their financial lives because of overspending. They hit their emotional and financial bottom because of their relationship with their work and earning. Recognizing that you need, want, and deserve more than your work is giving you can mark the beginning of transforming your relationship with work and earning. Asking yourself whether the money you earn allows you to meet your needs facilitates another layer of growth in your Financial Recovery. It is not surprising, then, that healing this relationship becomes the next step along the bridge of many people's Financial Recovery.

MY WORK STORY

A few months after opening my financial counseling business, things were going very well. Word of mouth was bringing me a steady stream of new clients. I loved my work and found it deeply satisfying. Business was good, but I was still living on a bare-bones spending plan. Given my history of not being able to manage my money, I naturally assumed that I still must be doing something wrong.

At about that time I decided to take a six-week course from a Bay Area therapist who was working with people on their money issues. At one point during this course I expressed the frustrations I was having about not being able to get ahead.

The therapist asked me what I was charging for my services, so I told her my hourly rate. She looked up at me and said, "You need to charge more." That took me by surprise. I had been so grateful to be out of the corporate life that didn't suit me and to be doing something that I loved that I'd never put the work and earning pieces together.

When I work with clients who have been using their spending plans effectively, they sometimes reach the same impasse. When I say to them, "You're doing great with your spending. You just don't make enough money," they respond with looks of relief and surprise.

Years after I'd connected the issues of work and earning, I was doing research to write *It's Your Money*. I sat on my office floor and went through all my client files. To my surprise, with rare exceptions, clients who had been working on their personal finances over a period of time had all increased their earnings. It didn't matter if they were self-employed or worked for a salary. They had all, as part of this process, changed something in their relationship with work and earning that caused them to earn more than they had when they had first come to see me.

Self-employed people and small-business owners had gotten better at charging appropriately and collecting their fees. Those on a salary had gotten assertive about seeking raises or had sought positions that compensated them for the real value of their work. Over and over, clients were able to apply what they'd learned about spending to what they were earning. They looked at their needs and determined that they deserved to be paid more for what they were doing.

It's so exciting when I see people begin to recognize that they deserve to have fulfilling work and to be appropriately compensated. What's important to note here is the sequence — the progression of this recovery process. If we are constantly struggling with managing our spending, more money alone won't fix that problem. However, once we have changed our relationship with spending, debt, and savings (as we've covered in the prior chapters), if a gap still remains between how we are living and how we want to live, looking at earning is the natural next step.

As you develop a firmer foundation of clarity and good money practices, it may be time for you to look at your relationship with work and earning. In the pages that follow, we'll see examples of how different people approach their relationship with work and earning. Though their specific professions and circumstances may be different from yours, I am sure you will find things in their stories that resonate with you.

As with so many issues that affect our relationships with money, it pays to look at not merely your current circumstances but also your history to learn how you developed your belief systems and attitudes about work and earning money.

ARE FAMILY HISTORY AND OLD MONEY MESSAGES INFLUENCING YOUR EARNING?

The events of our childhoods forcefully shape our lives, whether or not we are conscious of this force. I've come to learn that a troubled relationship with work and earning money can spring from our childhood experiences too. Exploring family history and the messages you absorbed from your early experiences can help you understand your current relationship with work and earning. It can also help you examine, with greater objectivity, whether your current work is working for you.

Some people have never asked themselves what they want from their work. Some devalue their skills or their capacities and feel they have to accept something less. Others grew up in affluent families, hobbled by the presence of family money. The knowledge that someone would always rescue them, by either gift or inheritance, became the cold water that squelched the fire in their bellies for making their own way in the world.

I've worked with people who grew up with modest means and who uncover feelings of guilt for wanting a financial life that is bigger than the one they grew up in. They minimize their desires for a bigger life, thinking themselves shallow or selfish. Those who have survived abusive, neglectful, or harshly critical family experiences often reveal untended wounds in their relationships with money, spending, and earning too.

No one would argue that our early family experiences have a lot to do with how we lead our lives, but many of us don't think about our relationship with work and earning as being connected to those experiences. Having role models who have a healthy relationship with money can be a crucial advantage. On the other hand, if money has been an area of struggle for you, it pays to look back at the experiences you had in your family concerning work and earning. What lessons did you learn from your family? Did you feel pressured or steered in any way? Asking yourself these kinds of questions can offer insights into not only your relationship with work but your lifelong relationship with money.

As you look at your relationship with money, you might discover vestiges of your family history: replication of patterns, adherence to expectations, or a stark rebellion against those messages. When it comes to our relationships with earning and the work we choose, family messages can also come to bear. Some money and work messages (both positive and negative) we hear in our families are overtly stated, such as the following:

- You can do whatever you want in life.
- Don't get too big for your britches.

- You can never make a living *that* way.
- You're lucky to have a job, so stick with it, no matter what.
- Job security is more important than job satisfaction.

Some of the messages we absorb from our families are never spoken out loud but might as well be posted on the refrigerator as family announcements. It might be fine if they stayed on the refrigerator, but they don't. Instead, we often carry them forward with us as we work to build our own work and financial lives.

For example, we might be shushed when we innocently ask how much money our parents make in their jobs. From this we might infer that there is something wrong with money or that it's not a subject we should explore. If we observe our parents or guardians go from boom to bust in their financial lives, we may learn that money is something we can never rely on. If our parents or guardians frequently pressure us to consider a certain profession, rather than supporting us to explore our own desires, we might conclude that only some choices will be met with family approval. The following exercise can help you understand the legacy your family left you regarding work and earning.

EXERCISE

Uncovering Family Messages about Work and Earning

I invite you to use your money journal to explore your own family history as it relates to work and earning. You may also find that it helps to discuss these questions with family members. Explore the following:

- What family messages about work and earning did you receive? Were they spoken or unspoken?

- Were you expected to do chores at home? How did you feel about that? Did you get paid? Describe.
- Did you receive an allowance? If so, how did you feel about your allowance? How did you manage your money? How was the amount determined?
- Were you paid for things other than doing chores (such as getting good grades, doing well in sports, or even keeping a secret)? Describe.
- What examples of relationships with work and earning were modeled for you ?
- What support, instruction, or encouragement were you given regarding work and earning?
- Did you feel free to explore professions different from those of your family members?
- Did you grow up feeling as though being either more or less financially successful would cause you to experience disapproval? Write about this.
- Was there family money that you were taught would take care of you? How did this affect your thoughts about work?
- What family stories about work and earning successes, failures, accomplishments, and so on did you hear about your family or people they knew?

Taking Inventory of How Work Has Been Working for You

Completing a Work History Inventory will help you explore how your decisions about work may have affected your entire approach to life. It can be an important step in identifying underearning issues. The process will help you discover your own definition of meaningful work and begin to create a vision for the lifestyle you *desire*. Once you explore that vision and match it with what you need to earn, you will be on the road to living the life you want to live.

EXERCISE

Your Work History Inventory

Reflect on your history and current circumstances in your relationship with work. You can make note of these reflections in your money journal. First of all, ask yourself this:

- What was your very first job as a kid? Was it a lemonade stand? A paper route? Babysitting? How did you feel the first time you earned money?

Next, create a list of every job you've ever had, in the order that you had them. Yes, all of them, whether they were paid or unpaid, part- or full-time, years ago or recent. To help you in this process I've included a free download of this exercise on my website (www.financialrecovery.com). For some people, this is quite a list. Think back to mowing the lawn, early fast-food jobs, and all the jobs you've had over the years. You may have had three different jobs all within the same company, so list those separately.

Once you've completed your list, write the title of each job at the top of a separate sheet of paper. If you have eighteen jobs on that initial list, you'll have eighteen sheets of paper. Then, thoughtfully answer the questions below about each job.

1. How did you get this job?
2. While you were doing this job, how did you feel about your work?
3. What skills did you use or develop in this job?
4. How much money did you earn?

5. How did you feel about the money that you earned? Did you feel you were paid what you deserved?
6. Why and how did you leave this job?
7. How much time did you have between this job and the next one?

When you are done answering the questions for every job, spread all your papers on a table or the floor and take some time to examine them. What do you notice and how do you feel when you see them all laid out together?

Now take a few deep breaths and then answer the following questions:

1. Which job(s) did you find most enjoyable, satisfying, and rewarding? Describe.
2. Which job(s) did you like least? Why?
3. Describe any patterns you notice regarding the types of jobs you've had.
4. Describe anything else you notice about your work and earning patterns.

IT'S ALWAYS FASCINATING TO SEE what comes up when people look at their Work History Inventory. It's just another angle from which to view and understand your relationship with money. It can be challenging for people who don't receive money for their work to think they can do this exercise. If you are a homemaker or work as a volunteer, it is equally useful to look at your work to understand your relationship with it.

While we tend to assume someone's income would go up with their work experience over time, some discover that they've fluctuated between good-paying jobs and ones that pay substantially less. Some observe that the long gaps between jobs have been a big part of their money problems, putting them into financial holes for years. I've had clients who realize they have a pattern of quitting or being fired from jobs, citing conflicts with bosses as the reason. Others have very few jobs in their history, noting that they stay in one place for a long time, whether or not they find the position and the money satisfying. I even had one student who noted, "I never noticed before that I've gotten nearly all my jobs because my mom helped me get them!"

Another client, in his midthirties, came to an appointment after doing this exercise. He was shocked to discover that he'd already had twenty-nine jobs since he'd graduated from college. More important, he saw in black and white that he had created a crisis in each one that had required him to leave — even when he had liked the work. Another client, a woman who was never able to make enough money at her jobs, recognized a pattern that had begun when the business where she had her very first job folded. She never even got her first paycheck.

This exercise isn't just a review of your résumé. It can be very useful for you to make notes about the patterns you observe in your relationship with work and earning. You might just be surprised by what you see.

As I mentioned earlier, Financial Recovery is about much more than the view in the rearview mirror (though in this case looking back does show us a lot). It's also about looking through the windshield at what is around us, and this next exercise will help you focus on how things are right now.

EXERCISE

Evaluating Your Current Work

Now shift your focus from the past to the present. Note your responses to the following:

1. How do you feel about your overall experience of the work you're currently doing? Is it fulfilling? Satisfying?

2. Is the stress level of the work you do manageable for you?
3. Are the hours you work compatible with your life?
4. Is the money you receive from your work adequate to meet your needs and provide the lifestyle you choose?
5. What (if any) changes do you imagine you might need to make in your relationship to work and earning for your professional life to be a source of satisfaction for you?
6. Do you have any secret or spoken fantasies about a profession or work style you'd prefer to the one you currently have?
7. Have you inherited money, or do you expect to inherit money? What are your feelings about that? How does this affect the decisions you make today?

By looking both to the past and to the present, you can gain a great deal of insight into your relationship with work over time and the patterns you've created. The next section will help you focus specifically on what works and what doesn't work in your current job.

Is Your Work Working for You?

At first, almost everyone with money struggles feels that more money will fix everything. Many find that once they've changed how they manage their money, they actually do earn enough to meet their needs and live in the way they want to live. In short, their work (and the money they earn) is working for them.

As you exit the survival mode of living in financial chaos and begin to feel the firm foundation of financial stability under your feet, I invite you to use this new vantage point to examine your relationship with work and the money it brings you. Is your work working for you? Are you bringing in enough money to live your life in the way you want to live it? Clients I have worked with generally describe their relationship with work and earning in one of the following three ways:

THE JOB WORKS — THE MONEY DOESN'T. They're content with their work, but the money is not adequate to meet their needs.

THE MONEY WORKS — THE JOB DOESN'T. The job pays well enough but is in other ways unsatisfying, is too stressful, or doesn't fit into how they want to live.

THE WORK DOESN'T WORK — NEITHER DOES THE MONEY. They hate their job and still are not making enough money!

Next we'll look at an example of each of these scenarios and what the person involved did to improve the situation. I hope that you can find within one of these stories inspiration to change your situation.

Joanna: The Job Works — The Money Doesn't

Joanna had worked for many years at a nonprofit organization that benefits children in her community. She loved her job and believed that the work done by her agency made an important difference in her community and in the lives of the kids they served. She lived debt-free and within her means, with a lot of creative efforts to get the most for her money. No matter how disciplined she was in her money management, Joanna just couldn't make her money stretch enough to live in the way she would like. She wanted to buy a home, and on her salary, this would be out of her reach. Joanna's work, even though she loved it, just wasn't working for her. She recognized that she was growing unhappy with the severe financial limitations that her "dream job" caused in her life.

Once she had spent some time looking at her family and work history and working with a spending plan to get in touch with her needs, Joanna realized that in order to have the life she wanted, she'd either have to get more money for the work she did or have to consider a career shift. The dilemma was that she was at the top salary that her position would pay.

Because she had learned to get creative in using her monthly spending plan, Joanna knew how much more she would need to earn to meet her needs and achieve her goals. She decided to apply some creativity to find a solution. She approached the director of her agency, with whom she had a great relationship, and presented her dilemma — as well as an idea. Perhaps if she could write and obtain a grant to expand the agency's services, she could get a promotion that would justify a raise in salary. The director had an even better idea. She didn't want to lose Joanna. She was planning to retire in two years and had been trying to figure out a way to cut back her hours in the meantime. She did some math and figured that if she went to four days a week instead of five and Joanna stepped into a codirector role, with the additional grant money, Joanna could increase her salary by 30 percent for the next two years. She'd also be well positioned to succeed the director when she retired, and that would mean another bump. It would take board approval and the new grant, but the plan made sense for all concerned.

Joanna's creativity and her rapport with her director were a big part of why this solution worked. However, Joanna's newfound awareness that she needed *and deserved* to make more money was what led her to address the situation and propose a plan to increase her salary.

Dianne: The Money Works — The Job Doesn't

Dianne worked as a counselor in the employee assistance department of a large bank. For twelve years she answered calls to the company's crisis hotline, helping callers manage various personal and professional crises. The calls covered workplace traumas such as bank robberies and mental health emergencies such as suicidal thoughts, family violence, and child abuse. Occasionally, Dianne even went into branches shortly after shootings and met with those who had witnessed the terrible events. She sometimes had to step over blood spatters to get to the frightened group that awaited her support. Dianne listened to literally hundreds of calls per year in which people described, in vivid detail, the most traumatic moments of their lives. Her empathy made her good at her work but it also made her vulnerable to the emotional stress that came with it.

While providing support to troubled callers gave Dianne great satisfaction, and the compensation she received eventually grew to be a six-figure salary, the emotional impact of her work became unbearable. She was unable to sleep. She felt raw at the end of each day, as though she were missing her outermost layer of skin, and she found that she could no longer tolerate watching the news or movies that had any element of intensity. Her work involved long hours and being on call overnight and on weekends. Her wrung-out emotional state and long hours made Dianne less available for her children's needs.

As she progressed in her Financial Recovery, Dianne and her husband began to see that some things were more important than a six-figure salary and the lifestyle it supported. After careful consideration, they decided that it would be best for Dianne to find a less stressful job. This necessitated some big changes for them. Their annual spending plan helped provide the information and insights they needed to make these changes without compromising their ability to meet their needs. They saw that by downsizing, selling their home, and moving to a less expensive community, they could live on a smaller income and be more available to their kids. Dianne developed a small private practice in her new community where she enjoyed the satisfaction of helping people but without the relentless exposure to trauma. She also developed a freelance writing career, and she loved being able to do this from home. Every day her young son came home from school and one or both of his parents were there to greet him.

Dianne and her husband reduced their income but adjusted their lives to make that income work. As a result, Dianne's work is now working for her.

James: The Work Doesn't Work — Neither Does the Money

Sometimes as we grow more aware of our relationship with money we come to understand the realistic limitations of what we are currently earning. James's earnings fell far short of giving him what he needed. He was very unhappy with his work and his financial circumstances. When I met him, he was just at the beginning of making big changes in his relationship with work and earning.

James's financial story had nothing to do with overspending or any other form of excess. In fact, he was living in a serious state of deprivation. He was working for a car dealership earning $800 a month, plus commission. Unfortunately, since he could never seem to actually sell a car, there were no commissions. Half of his income went toward the rent at his friend's apartment where he was staying temporarily. At a certain point, the desperation James felt became overwhelming. "I'm sick and tired of not having any money. I can't keep living this way," he thought. He realized in that moment that he was willing to do whatever it took "not to be poor anymore."

The irony was that James was a licensed attorney with ten years of experience. Earlier he had bought a small private law practice and had tried to run it on his own. Despite his skills as an attorney and his charm and intelligence, James lacked the skills and the temperament to operate a business. Eventually, it became clear that the business was doomed to fail. James was able to sell what was left of the practice and lived off that money for a short while. Soon, because he'd always loved cars, he thought that by selling them he could make ends meet while he determined his next steps. After months of working hard, James had not sold a single car. He was in a state of emotional and spiritual crisis. Completely unsure how to go forward, James hit a financial, emotional, and spiritual low. He felt desperate and lost, his self-esteem crushed. He was not overspending; his issue was that he had inadequate resources for supporting himself — he was underearning. His relationship to work and earning was ruining his life.

By working the Financial Recovery process and looking at his Work History Inventory, James eventually determined that it was not the field of law that hadn't worked for him; it was running his own practice. He was by nature not entrepreneurial, and it was a better fit for him to be employed by a firm. Once he saw this, he was able to look for and find a position with an established firm that allowed him to earn a wage that was satisfying for him. James created a financially healthy lifestyle in which he could meet his needs.

IF YOU ARE UNHAPPY IN YOUR JOB for any reason — whether it is because the job is too stressful, is unsatisfying, or doesn't pay enough to meet your needs — you may want to consider a change. This may involve getting in touch with your own skills, talents, and desires and looking, as Joanna did, for a creative way to make your current work *work* for you. Or, as in Dianne's case, it may involve being bold and creative and changing jobs so that your work can become a source of satisfaction rather than something that is doing you harm. Other times it requires honestly evaluating your needs as well as your talents and professional skills, as James did.

Remember to explore what you can realistically expect to earn in a given job. Here is where your annual spending plan can really help you. If you are applying the skills of Financial Recovery to your life, you'll have better clarity about your own needs and how much money is required to meet them. This will allow you to better assess whether the income that comes with the work you want will allow you to have the lifestyle you want.

WHAT IS YOUR EARNING CEILING?

In earlier chapters when we talked about the Money/Life Drain, I challenged you to look at the patterns in your spending. Now it's time to look with that same eye at the earning side of your relationship with money. This process will help you become aware of the limiting beliefs you might have about your earning potential. You have the power to either act on or change whatever patterns or limiting beliefs you uncover. Through your monthly spending plan and especially through your annual spending plan, you create the vision for the lifestyle you desire and the cost of that lifestyle. It makes sense to have your earnings match what you've designed in your planning, and this process can help you get there.

I've done the exercise below with clients as well as students at workshops for many years. The insights are often very revealing and can give you a great deal of information about your relationship to earning.

In the workshops, I take participants through what I call the Earning Ceiling Meditation. It's a guided meditation in which I encourage them to visualize different levels of earning. I ask them to close their eyes and imagine themselves in a great job that they enjoy and are very good at. Then I ask them to imagine that they are being paid $25,000 a year to do this job that they love. I ask, "How do you feel about your job? How do you feel about the earnings?" I instruct them to imagine what it would feel like to earn this amount of money. What do they feel? What do they notice?

Then, still with their eyes closed, I say that I've raised their annual earnings to $50,000. What does this feel like? I move to $75,000. As I raise the amount to higher and higher numbers, the atmosphere in the room starts to change. I've learned to read the signs of when people have reached their "earning ceiling." This is the amount above which they don't believe they could ever earn.

You may think you don't have an earning ceiling, but every time I've done this exercise, every person I've done it for has found his or her limit. At some point the tension of trying to visualize themselves earning a particular level of salary proves too much. Reactions vary, but the most common reaction I've seen is that when they reach their limit, people's eyes pop open and I'm greeted with a "you've got to be kidding" look. I continue to raise the earning level to $150,000, then $200,000. Sometimes by now people are fidgeting or even snickering. Depending on the group, I continue to go up in increments, sometimes getting as high as a million dollars, and sometimes beyond. By that point very few people, if any, remain with their eyes closed.

EXERCISE

Finding Your Earning Ceiling

It's journal time again (I know, there's a lot of deep work in this chapter, but it's very rewarding on many levels). I want you to take yourself through this visualization. If you'd find it helpful to record this on a form, you can download the Earning Ceiling Meditation form from my website (www.financialrecovery.com).

If you're using your money journal, write earning levels down in $25,000 increments starting at $25,000 and going as high as you would like. After each amount write answers to the following questions:

1. How does it feel to earn this amount of money?
2. What do you notice about yourself at this income level?
3. What attitudes come up as you contemplate making this amount of money?

When you have fully visualized yourself at that level, move on to the next income level. Keep going up until you reach a level where you just can't imagine yourself making that much money. Where did you get this belief? Is it based on facts or just assumed?

When I take people through this visualization and ask them how it felt to reach their own ceiling I often hear answers such as these:

- I couldn't earn that much because I'd have to work too hard.
- It would be too much responsibility to be at that level.
- I'd have to give up too much to make that happen.
- That would be impossible for me.
- I'd have to be ruthless to get that, and I'm not willing to compromise my values.

These same phrases come up for different people at different levels of earning. People with very different income ceilings and different career histories often talk about similar internal blocks and concerns when they think of making more money. Is it their resistance to the amount of money, or does it stem from deeper beliefs born of their individual family histories?

When you have found your earning ceiling, remember, you can break through it. The first time I did this exercise it was hard to believe I would ever make enough money to break through that ceiling. But I did. So did James, and Joanna. If you want to break through that imaginary earning ceiling, you'll need to first identify that it exists for you, then determine what it would take to break through it. For some, this is about confidence. For others, it's about overcoming negative assumptions about what it might mean to make that much money. Identifying your imagined earning ceiling and altering your beliefs about it could require some outside support. Qualified therapists, career counselors, and especially certified Financial Recovery counselors can be mentors who help you through this part of the process.

Looking at our history of earning and combining it with understanding our assumptions about what our personal earning ceiling might be can tell us a lot about the patterns and internally held belief systems that might be keeping us from earning the money we say we want. Remember, this is about a progression. Those who are walking the bridge of Financial Recovery don't necessarily start addressing these work and earning issues right away (though some do). At some point, though, the process you are going through will lead you to ask these questions to begin to see how your earnings fit in with your spending plan and determine if it's time for a change.

I want to share with you the story of a couple whose process demonstrates perfectly how this can work in your own recovery.

CASE STUDY
Catherine and Michael

I recently interviewed Catherine and Michael, former clients whom I've seen off and on over several years. They talked about all they'd accomplished during the years of healing their relationship with money. All the changes they'd made, and the consciousness they'd developed by practicing Financial Recovery, had created a turning point in their relationship with their work and their marriage as well.

When Catherine and Michael first came to see me, both of them were struggling in their relationship with money. Their money issues played out in their marriage too, and they were at a crucial turning point. Throughout their marriage, Michael had received a series of small inheritances, little windfalls that had dug them out of one or another financial predicament. These little windfalls had allowed Michael to continue as an underearner for years. He had recently received what he knew was to be the last of these inheritances.

Catherine was sick of their never-ending financial troubles. While she wanted to continue as a stay-at-home mom, she recognized that without the promise of another inheritance, they could not live on Michael's salary. Michael and Catherine agreed to come into financial counseling because they knew that their relationship with work and earning had to change.

Michael and Catherine were both in recovery from addiction and understood the value of committing to a course to overcome their patterns. "Money is the thing that always slipped through our shared recovery process," Michael explained.

The couple confessed to just how vulnerable their marriage was. One day after leaving my office, Michael had told Catherine, "We're screwed. I just know you're going to leave me."

"It goes back to a family pattern with money," Michael

explained. "There were people who only wanted to be around me because I had go-carts and things. If I hadn't had those things they wouldn't have wanted me." Michael expressed his vulnerable feeling that Catherine wouldn't want him if he couldn't support her. "If I didn't have the bucks, there was no point. I didn't feel I had any value without money," he said.

Over many months of working together, the couple built a spending plan and began reducing debt and growing savings. "We were on the same page. We were both present," Michael said. Overcoming their initial resistance, they embraced money consciousness. They practiced tracking and adjusting their spending plan to keep themselves aligned with their goals.

Catherine explained, "I always tell people that in Financial Recovery I learned how to be a grown-up when it came to money. One thing that became clear through this process was that we were not making enough money. We'd been enabling our underearning with these inheritances, and we'd never had to address the real issue of work and income before."

At the time, Michael operated a small piano sales and restoration business out of a warehouse. He revealed that he'd always dreamed of owning a family business, one in which he and Catherine could work together. Catherine grew willing to share in a venture with him, but she'd gotten clear about her own needs too. She was unwilling to work in a warehouse.

The couple then had a remarkable opportunity cross their path. A small piano store came up for sale. It was priced right, was in an ideal location, and came with the perfect line of quality pianos. Because of their work improving their individual and shared relationship with money, their personal finances were stable. Both were able to recognize the opportunity for what it was.

Michael and Catherine bought their piano store in 2007, just prior to the recession that crushed so many businesses. They operated the business with the same principles they'd learned in their personal finances. They kept the business lean, staying in touch with spending and keeping their needs clear. They made a business spending plan and stuck to it by making thoughtful adjustments and planning for the unexpected. Even their bookkeeper was impressed with the way they operated and tracked the progress of their business.

Though the recession kept Michael and Catherine's piano store from growing as fast as they'd first hoped, their solid practices helped the business survive while so many others were closing their doors. They've kept the business small and basic, but it's remained secure and profitable.

For Michael and Catherine, as for many people, developing their relationship with work and earning was a natural step in the progression of their work in Financial Recovery. Once they were no longer in survival mode, living from one inheritance check to the next, they were able to recognize and seize a business opportunity. They'd created a sound financial foundation, and this allowed them to design a work life that worked for them. As a result of their hard work, Catherine and Michael not only improved their financial lives and created a satisfying business but strengthened the foundation of their relationship as well. This was an added and invaluable payoff of Michael and Catherine's Financial Recovery.

THE PITFALLS OF INHERITANCES, WINDFALLS, AND SUDDEN WEALTH

Some who grow up with privilege are also endowed with a sense of direction, inspiration, and personal responsibility that helps them find their way in the world. Others who grow up with the same financial resources are not as endowed with emotional and practical skills. They are, in fact, limited by the presence of money, lacking confidence in their ability to make their own way in the world. I've worked with people who, well into adulthood, have remained completely dependent on their parents and have found no meaningful relationship with work of their own. Some have blown great fortunes, thinking them infinite, only to find that there is a bottom to what once seemed like an endless well of money.

Michael's small inheritances came intermittently. They didn't provide enough to eliminate the necessity of working, but they were enough to enable his life of underearning. Rather than creating a work life that provided adequately for his and his family's needs, he and Catherine used the inherited money as a replacement for low income. It's easy to fall into this trap.

Sudden bursts of income sound like good things — who wouldn't want a sudden influx of money? But they can be obstacles to a healthy relationship with work and earning, especially for those who are unprepared for the windfall's impact. Those unaccustomed to having large sums at their disposal may spend wildly until suddenly the money is gone. We've seen this in highly publicized cases of celebrities and professional athletes. From *Survivor* champions to rookie basketball players to sweepstakes winners, even the wealthiest are not immune. Losing a fortune can bring enormous shame. When this shame is made public, it adds stinging humiliation. These people often experience the harsh judgment of others who can't understand how someone with so much could end up broke.

The problem with windfalls, in whatever form, is that they can skew our perspective on work and earning money. Sadly, some people see windfalls as their financial plan. Despite all reasonable odds, they live in a state of magical thinking and operate their financial lives assuming that they'll be rescued by an unexpected infusion of cash. Some believe that their next "big deal" will save them. Others imagine that winning the lottery or becoming the next American Idol will pull them out of their financial binds. Living as though something is magically going to fix their situations keeps many people caught in the Money/Life Drain.

It is never a good idea to bank on a possible future windfall or to consider such money events as a viable plan. Winning lottery tickets are extremely rare — and a terrible financial plan. Sometimes inheritances are less than anticipated or don't come at all. Maybe Grandpa decided to leave all his money to charity or lost it all to bad investments. Booms go bust and bonuses dwindle when the economy tanks. Sometimes those raises, commissions, or bonuses that we're expecting don't come our way after all. And by the time we realize this, we are trapped in the Money/Life Drain. You can avoid this situation by providing for your own needs through your monthly and annual spending plans.

Should You Be an Entrepreneur or an Employee?

Many struggle with self-employment. A great idea or the love of a certain line of work may have inspired them to start a business. However, the running of the business doesn't work for them. They find themselves hating what they do and not earning enough money at it anyway. Others feel constrained working in jobs that don't suit them, yearning for the freedom that they imagine a business of their own would provide.

Whether you are an entrepreneur or a salaried employee, it's important that you make an accurate assessment of how you can work most successfully. Some people have the entrepreneurial bent. The work required to grow and operate a business of their own causes them to thrive. They love it, and they succeed. Those for whom being an employee fits better feel much more comfortable getting a steady paycheck.

Your Work History Inventory will help you see which work style works best for you. There is nothing inherently better in either being self-employed or being employed by others. It's just necessary to know which works for you.

Don't Let Self-Employment Become Self-Imprisonment

For those who don't find contentment in traditional jobs and those who have entrepreneurial skills, being self-employed can be a great option. If self-employment or operating your own business is right for you, it can be a great way to design your own way of working and creating a satisfying relationship with work. But there is a danger here: not everyone is suited to self-employment, and the skill set for doing a job (even a highly skilled one) can be quite different from the skills it takes to operate a business from day to day.

I've noticed that my client base over the years has reflected a preponderance of small business owners and self-employed people. Those who are self-employed face some special money challenges. While self-employment was a great fit for Michael and Catherine, James realized he was not suited to running a practice. Instead, he could better utilize his skills at a firm where he could focus on being an attorney without being a business owner. Owning a business can bring both great freedoms and big challenges, and self-employed people have another dimension of exploration to do to understand their relationship with work and earning.

Being self-employed can also contribute mightily to unhappiness and stress. In this case, you could find yourself no longer self-employed but self-imprisoned. Work and earning issues can figure strongly for the self-employed. If you are spending your time and energy running a business and you are not making enough profit to meet your needs, it is going to be very difficult to have a spending plan that works well for you.

As I have worked with clients who are self-employed, I have discovered a couple of things that are important in operating your own business successfully and happily.

SEE THE WORK AS A BUSINESS. Many self-employed people have a hard time viewing their work as a business. They often undercharge or have difficulty collecting fees. Their sliding scales sometimes slide too far. Consultants and contractors have a hard time bidding accurately for their jobs in a way that is profitable and values their time. Hair stylists, landscapers, and website designers end up doing work for friends at little or no charge.

While there is nothing wrong with helping family and friends, it's useful to remember that if you've developed skills that people want, it pays to value these skills appropriately. If you can help a friend or loved one, that's great. Just remain mindful that you also deserve to have the time and energy to put into your business so that you can earn the money you need.

APPLY FINANCIAL RECOVERY PRINCIPLES IN YOUR BUSINESS. The skills of sorting needs from wants, having a spending plan, and tracking your money are just as useful in a business as they are in your personal life. This is especially true for those who freelance or bid work (such as contractors and landscapers). If you're carefully monitoring your money and tracking expenses, you will be able to see which jobs are profitable and which just eat your time, energy, and money. On top of that, your bookkeeper and tax accountant will love you!

Challenges for Those Employed by Others

While working for someone else may rid you of many of the hassles of self-employment, traditional jobs can have their challenges as well. Many people who work in this way adopt a belief that they're stuck or that they are unable to change the things that don't work about their jobs. The following suggestions might help you avoid the traps into which salaried workers sometimes fall.

DON'T FORGET TO ASK FOR RAISES. Many people assume that it's impossible to get a raise. They may go years without approaching their bosses about increasing their salary.

BE CAREFUL NOT TO OVERDO OVERTIME. Working lots of overtime is one of those things that can creep up on you. If you're regularly working excessive amounts of overtime without getting paid for it, this is actually reducing your hourly wage. Depending on the requirements of your job, you might want to consider trying to limit your overtime or seeking compensation for it.

THINK EXPANSIVELY. If you need a higher salary, you might want to look beyond the traditional raise as your only option. Perhaps you can negotiate a new position within your organization. If you offer your boss a plan, you might just be surprised by what happens.

DON'T ASSUME THAT YOU'RE STUCK. It's always a challenge to think about changing jobs, but if your job is a source of excessive stress, or if it does not pay you what your work is worth, it may be time to consider a move. Naturally, you'll want to factor in the current job market before making any changes.

Your relationship with work and earning is a valuable component of developing a healthy relationship with money. Looking to what you earn and how you feel about it is a natural outgrowth of your work in Financial Recovery. Understanding that you have value and deserve to have that value rewarded is a wonderful feeling, one that I hope this process helps bring to you, and that you can pass on to those you love.

The Next Generation: You're Creating Your Kids' Family Money History

When people first arrive in my office for financial counseling, many of them are very focused on providing for their kids' futures. They're thinking about college funds and weddings. Of course, all good parents think about providing for their kids. I often have to help people slow down and focus on their current financial circumstances as part of building for their kids' futures. By getting their current finances on track, they can begin to build toward a stable future, and this means providing for their kids too. One of the best things you can do for your children's financial future is to be a model for them.

When we model for our children a healthy relationship with money and help them understand the relationship between work and earning money right from the beginning, we are giving them the most valuable kind of inheritance. We endow them with the confidence in their own abilities. We give them an inheritance of sound money management. We support them in making wise and informed choices about the work they choose and the lifestyle that fits them.

It's also important that we tune in to our kids — help them

see the value of knowing what they truly need. By both modeling and talking openly with them, we can help them understand the lure of wants and the power of advertising.

In their relationship with their kids, a lot of parents underestimate their impact as their children's first career counselors. By seeing our children for the special and unique individuals that they are, we can better support them in choosing a profession that is right for them, rather than the one that we want them to have. Ultimately, this will help them be happier and more satisfied in their own lives.

With our own solid relationships with money in place, we are free to look beyond just getting and managing our money. We begin to look to money as a tool that we can use to enrich our lives and the lives of our families on an even deeper level.

CHAPTER EIGHT

Imagining Sterling Money Behaviors

Claiming the Life You Were Meant to Live

> *Success means having the courage, the determination,*
> *and the will to become the person you believe*
> *you were meant to be.*
>
> — GEORGE SHEEHAN

As you gain more clarity and awareness in your relationship with money, the vision of how you want to live your life continues to emerge. The life you deserve and were meant to live becomes clearer and more attainable. As the financial fog clears and money crises are no longer a constant force, you're better able to see what is truly and deeply important to you — what you value most. The path from where you are to where you want to be grows more apparent, and you are able to determine the steps you have to take to get there.

In most programs about money, the only way you'd measure your success would be mathematically. Account balances. Asset values. Net worth. Quantifying these elements of your financial life is an important part of marking your financial progress. But that's not the whole story of Financial Recovery.

As you begin to accomplish your financial goals and meet your needs along the way, an amazing thing starts to happen. Not only do you develop a healthy relationship with money, but you also develop a healthier, more respectful, and nurturing relationship with yourself. By honoring your needs, you are acting in a self-respectful way — in other words, valuing yourself.

People are often surprised at the big impact little changes have on their lives. By creating a ritual to pay bills on time, you eliminate the heart-racing and humiliating experience of getting phone calls from creditors. Because you have a spending plan in place, you can rest your head on your pillow each night and fall asleep thinking about something other than money worries.

You may need to tune in to recognize these subtler milestones of Financial Recovery, but please do. The emotional, psychological, and spiritual residuals of this program are as vital as account balances in the measure of the success of your process. These are the *unquantifiable* experiences that add to your quality of life.

FROM SHAKY TO STABLE

At some point during each person's Financial Recovery process, a special thing happens. I experienced this personally and have witnessed it many times with clients over the years. This is when the person suddenly realizes, "Wow! I'm doing it! This is actually working!"

You've begun using the tools that cause the Money/Life Drain to lose much of its pull, and its force is replaced with confidence that the steps you're taking are changing your life in a profound way. This feeling occurs at different moments for different people. It might happen when you notice you no longer avoid the mailbox in fear of late notices and bills, when you enjoy your first-ever guilt-free vacation, or when you're suddenly able to consider working less so that you can spend more time doing what you'd like to do.

When you experience these moments — whatever they look and feel like for you — you'll notice the progress you're making and that some areas of your life are starting to feel less shaky. You're starting to enjoy the beginnings of financial stability. Things may not be easy, but the outcomes you hope for begin to seem possible.

To some, the idea of being stable in their relationship with money doesn't sound like a big deal. But for those of us who have lived in financial chaos and the fear and shame that come with it (whether because of circumstances outside our control or those we've generated by our own choices), *stable* can feel pretty darned great! This stability is part of the life you are meant to live, and it has resulted because you've put the principles of Financial Recovery into action. Let's review what you've learned about how to create financial health and well-being:

- You've learned to discern between needs and wants and to recognize when you're making inadequate substitutions. These substitutions don't meet your needs, and they cause you to experience an emotional or financial state of deprivation.

- You've become conscious of and connected to your money and spending behaviors by tracking every transaction, thereby knowing where your money goes.

- You recognize that chronic money problems are typically not isolated events but result from patterns of overspending, underearning, or chronic debting that lead to the experience of the Money/Life Drain.

- You've taken a hard look at your relationship with money, assessing the reality of your current circumstances, patterns, and money behaviors. You've come out of the financial fog, secrecy, and isolation. You've looked at where you are and what you want to accomplish in your financial life.

- You've worked to replace self-recrimination and shame with positive actions that will help restore (or create for the first time) a sense of confidence, pride, and self-esteem.
- By planning one month at a time, you've begun to take care of your needs and obligations in a realistic and do-able way.
- You know how to make adjustments to your spending plan, creating flexibility to allow for unanticipated events.
- You understand how to save your way out of debt, and you use periodic and safety-net savings to keep debt from recurring.
- You're evaluating your relationship with work and money. You continue to examine how your income and your work are, or are not, meeting your needs and bringing you closer to fulfilling your goals.

This stability is part of the life you are meant to live, and it has resulted because you've put the principles of Financial Recovery into action. You're living according to what I call "My Financial Recovery Declaration" (see page 241), which summarizes the principles and practices of this program. You might find it helpful to photocopy this page and post it on a wall or your refrigerator or keep it in your wallet, desk, or car. Whenever you need a reminder of the financial life you're working toward and how to get there, you'll know exactly where to look.

A WAY OF LIFE, NOT A SINGLE DESTINATION

It's important to remember that Financial Recovery isn't a single destination, a place at which we arrive with a grand ta-da, then plop down, thinking, "Whew! Glad that work is all over."

Some people make the mistake of thinking that once the pain

MY FINANCIAL RECOVERY DECLARATION

- I can discern between my needs and my wants. I recognize when I'm making inadequate substitutions. These substitutions don't meet my needs, and they cause me to experience emotional, spiritual, or financial deprivation.
- I have become conscious of and connected to my money and spending behaviors by tracking every transaction, thereby knowing where my money goes.
- I understand that chronic money problems are typically not isolated events but result from patterns of overspending, underearning, or chronic debting and that these patterns lead to the experience of the Money/Life Drain. I am conscious of my past unhealthy patterns and committed to cultivating and sustaining healthy patterns in my financial life from now on.
- I have taken a hard look at my relationship with money, assessing the reality of my current circumstances and money behaviors. I have come out of the financial fog, secrecy, and isolation. I have identified what I want to accomplish in my financial life.
- I have worked to replace self-recrimination and shame with positive actions that will help restore (or create for the first time) a sense of confidence, pride, and self-esteem.
- By planning one month at a time I have begun to take care of my needs and obligations in a realistic and doable way.
- I know how to make adjustments to my spending plan, creating flexibility to allow for unanticipated events.
- I understand how to save my way out of debt, and I use periodic and safety-net savings to keep debt from recurring.
- I am evaluating my relationship with work and money. I continue to examine whether my income and work are meeting my needs and bringing me closer to fulfilling my goals.

of financial crisis has subsided, it's no longer necessary to track spending or create monthly spending plans. They may think they've "arrived" at financial health. In reality, it's vital to continue these practices. Without them, before you know it, you can slip back into the old money behaviors that gave the Money/Life Drain all its power. To prevent this, be on the lookout for the following red flags, which indicate that you might be slipping back into old, detrimental ways:

· Resuming the use of credit cards
· Losing track of your account balances
· Neglecting to track your spending and earning
· Failing to create your monthly spending plans
· Resuming secret spending

It's easy to get discouraged if you find yourself slipping into old patterns of money behavior. You might then drift into the "oh wells." You might feel so bad about not doing everything perfectly that you abandon the healthy money behaviors you've begun. Then the whole cycle starts again.

If this happens, it's especially important to exercise compassion and patience toward yourself. Remember how it felt to first have clarity and come out of the vagueness of financial fog? Look at yourself with caring eyes, as you would anyone who is struggling to learn and grow.

On any path of personal growth — whether it's adopting a healthier diet, creating or maintaining strong personal relationships, or being on a course of spiritual growth and discovery — the journey is never just a straight, uninterrupted line. We don't learn a lesson, apply it, and move on. If this were the case, there would be a lot of therapists, fitness trainers, and financial counselors with absolutely nothing to do. Instead, progress is commonly punctuated with minor setbacks. It can be frustrating when we catch ourselves slipping into old and sometimes self-defeating patterns, but it's deeply human to do so. When this happens, the most productive response is to notice that you're slipping, to waste as little time as possible flogging yourself with guilt, shame, and self-recrimination, and to get yourself back on track. Rereading the Financial Recovery Declaration can help bring you back from the brink of "oh well" thinking.

The beauty of the Financial Recovery skills and practices is that they remain your tools for a lifetime. The simple steps of tracking, creating spending plans, and making adjustments to your plan work to help you build a healthy relationship with money, maintain that relationship, and get back on track if you find old patterns returning.

> *Fall down seven times,*
> *get up eight times.*
> — JAPANESE PROVERB

I've witnessed over and over again that taking positive action is the very best way to get back on track. As you make these actions habits, gradually your successes build on one another until they form a new and lasting pattern of financial health and well-being. Motivation may come and go, but the habits built in Financial Recovery will continue to pay off. Again, it's about trusting this process — and yourself.

EXERCISE

Defining and Creating Financial Health

Just as you plan a trip with a clear image of a destination in mind, it's important to define where your journey toward financial health will lead you. That way you'll be able to identify the experience when you get there. By defining what financial health means for you, you'll be better able to recognize it as you achieve it and to appreciate it in an ongoing way. In your journal, take a few moments to write answers to the questions below.

- How do I define financial health and stability?
- What needs to be in place for me to feel that I have a solid foundation in my financial life?
- When I have this foundation, how will I feel? How will I act?
- What are friends and loved ones noticing about me and the new way I'm living in my relationship with money?
- What is it like to know that I am able to meet my needs now and will continue doing so into the future?

As you continue to progress through the stages of Financial Recovery, you can revisit what you've written. To do so will be both a measure of your progress toward your goals and your opportunity to add new dimensions to the vision you're creating for yourself. If you find yourself losing confidence along the way, the descriptions you write, along with the Financial Recovery Declaration, can serve as a trail of bread crumbs that helps you find your way back to your path of financial health.

A CLEAR DEFINITION OF FINANCIAL HEALTH provides a standard by which you can evaluate your money choices. Are you treating yourself well? Are you treating yourself as you would want your best friend or most treasured loved one to treat herself? Each time you encounter a spending opportunity or money decision you'll be able to ask yourself: *Is this a life-enhancing expenditure that will bring me closer to my financial health? Or is this in any way a life-damaging expenditure that undermines my course or does me harm?*

As you move forward in this state of financial health, you'll continue to shape and hone your successful money practices.

I tend to think of this phase of Financial Recovery as a sort of graduate school. You've mastered the elementary principles, but you continue to discover new depths of understanding. You find clever ways to trim excesses from your plan so that you can have more of what you want and need or can meet goals that you have determined. You apply greater creativity to meeting your needs and learn on deeper levels what real satisfaction means for you.

> *It is never too late to be what you might have been.*
> — GEORGE ELIOT

You continue to define the terms of living an expansive life. Whatever these moments of insight and peace are for you, they are evidence of your growth. I invite you to experience them with elation and a sense of accomplishment. After all, you've made this happen.

When it comes to Financial Recovery, healing occurs right from the beginning as you start to change your behavior and use the tools. Health comes when you sustain those practices over time. But that's not where the possibilities stop. As you continue this process, more and more exciting possibilities will emerge.

UNANTICIPATED BENEFITS OF FINANCIAL RECOVERY

For many, the experience of obtaining a satisfying level of financial health and well-being is marked with something quite surprising — an unfamiliar quiet and the sense that they can breathe deeply for the first time in a very long time. Gone is the noise of the telephone ringing during dinner with relentless hounding from creditors. Quieted are thoughts of self-recrimination and worry. Stilled is the constant drone of mental calculations and schemes devised just to try, in vain, to make ends meet.

The practical consequences of financial health can be quantified by looking at account balances. You can measure that things are moving from shaky to stable. Bills are paid. You may have started saving for the first time in your life. Flickers of hope for a stable (and even abundant) financial future are not only in the imagination — they are becoming a reality.

But the *emotional benefits* that come with Financial Recovery are beyond measure. You can live without money secrets. You no longer have to live under the shadow of shame or fear. You will no longer be haunted by the ghosts of your financial past and the constant ache of feeling that the future holds no hope. Perhaps for the first time, you'll be free of the fear that you're about to be punished for some invisible crime and the looming threat of some enormous penalty.

I've heard clients at this stage of our work together say things like, "I can't believe it, but I never worry about money anymore." (By the way, I've heard this from people all along the income spectrum.) Clients have said, "I can finally sleep at night," and "I feel so proud that I am able to do this for myself and my family." I've heard many versions of "I don't feel like I'm just surviving anymore. I'm really living."

One of the most deeply satisfying discoveries people make along this journey is that they start to feel as though the tasks of tracking, planning, and remaining conscious of and connected to their money are not just obligations. Instead, these behaviors begin to feel self-nurturing, evidence of a new kind of self-regard. "I *deserve* to take care of myself. I *deserve* the rewards of financial stability. I *deserve* to claim the life I was meant to live." These emotional dividends are the priceless riches that come from this process of healing.

CHANGE THAT SUSTAINS

At the beginning of this book I acknowledged that Financial Recovery is not a quick fix or a get-rich-quick program. I think of this as one of the most positive aspects of this process. Changes that come quickly are often short lived because there's no time to learn at a really deep level what it takes to sustain them. This sets people up to repeat the problem behaviors again and again. But when genuine transformation comes as a result of efforts sustained over time, learning takes place on a significantly deeper level. That learning sticks with us.

By doing the work of Financial Recovery, staying conscious of your relationship with money in an ongoing, daily way, you'll elevate your choices into ritual. This creates change that is sustainable over time. Yes, it will sometimes be challenging. Yes, you'll likely experience setbacks. Often you'll want things to happen faster than they do. But what you'll gain along the way is vital. You'll develop an increasing awareness of both your head and your heart as you make financial decisions — honoring what is practical while still staying in touch with your deepest physical, emotional, and spiritual needs. You'll

> *Perseverance is not a long race; it is many short races one after another.*
> — **WALTER ELLIOTT**

gain self-knowledge about your relationship with money, and when you have that, your integrity, confidence, and sense of your own value will continue to grow.

DEFINING "ENOUGH"

Lots of us think we have a pretty good idea of what "not enough" means when it comes to money. Not enough to pay our bills. Not enough to do what we want to do. Not enough to have all that we want. Many clients come to financial counseling because even though they are working hard, they feel that the illusive "enough" will never come to them.

By learning to relate to their money in healthier, more strategic ways, many people discover that their financial resources go a lot farther than they ever thought possible. Even with the added expense of financial counseling and no increase in their income, many clients find that because they are planning their spending and remaining connected to their money choices, they really do have enough to meet their needs with what they already have. "Enough," to me, means sufficient means to meet your needs without overdoing in unnecessary or harmful ways. Evaluating how you're generating money and whether the amount of time required is in keeping with the rest of what you value is also part of determining whether you truly have "enough."

> We work to become,
> not to acquire.
> — ELBERT HUBBARD

FROM STABLE TO STERLING

Once freed of the distractions of financial turmoil, people frequently experience clarity and a sense of freedom and playfulness. This is often a stage of great creativity — a time to let your imagination wander and invite visions of how you see your life growing and expanding. I've suggested throughout this book that keeping a journal can be a great asset to your Financial Recovery process, and we've used it for several exercises to support your recovery.

What appeared on a page of my journal one day in 1999, years into my own Financial Recovery journey, was a question: What would *sterling* money behaviors look like for me?

Sterling? The word stuck in my mind, and I reflected on it. I realized at that point that I wanted my relationship with money to be elevated to another level. Learning to have a healthy relationship with money saved me in a thousand ways. But *sterling* meant something beyond healthy.

Sterling brought to mind images of refinement, clarity, and elegance — the highest standard of excellence. Practicing sterling money behaviors, then, means that all my financial interactions reflect the person I am striving to be and gradually becoming. The scars of my old experiences will remain in my memory, but I can nonetheless practice sterling money behaviors in the present.

Admittedly, the qualities of sterling money behaviors are challenging to define and to measure. I was recently looking through one of my favorite books about home design, *A Passion for Detail* by Charlotte Moss. There are plenty of design books filled with pictures of beautiful furnishings and well-executed design. But what makes this book, and this designer, inspirational is that Moss looks beyond just the beautiful artifacts she places in a room. She looks beyond the design techniques of balance, symmetry, scale, and color to the less tangible qualities she wishes to create. Moss also considers the experience she wants for those who enter the rooms she designs. She says, "I never leave a room I'm working on until it contains comfort, passion, and humor."[1] These words represent Moss's values in design. They are the intangible but oh-so-valuable aspects of what she's creating, and they serve as her own measure of excellence. They are her words, her definitions.

It's for you to identify the intangible *qualities* of sterling money behavior in your own life. As you think about sterling money behaviors, it can be useful to think of the various aspects of your life: your spiritual life, family, physical health, emotional well-being, friendships, business partnerships, and relationship with your community. You might, for example, want to be a model of financial health to your children or to exemplify integrity, fairness, and healthy generosity to your business associates or employees. Perhaps you want to create enough financial security that you can work less and have more time to spend with loved ones or to devote to the activities and causes that matter most to you. It's about what you value. How you obtain money, as well as where you invest your resources — your time, energy, and money — reflects what you value most.

Sterling money behaviors can exist right from the beginning of the Financial Recovery process. But imagining sterling behaviors and an ideal life is admittedly far easier once you've created stability in your financial affairs. Without crisis, panic, guilt, and shame, your imagination is freer to think more about your ideals, your values, and the quality of life you want to lead as well as the quantity of money you'll need to lead it.

I invite you to envision what sterling money behaviors might look like for you. How would it feel to practice those behaviors? Where would you invest your time, your energy, and your money? What rewards would you want to enjoy?

The following exercise can help you add more detail to the idea of sterling money behaviors and what it means to you.

EXERCISE

Create the Life You Desire — and Deserve

Put yourself in an environment that is conducive to reflection and imagination. For some people that means being alone in nature and for others it means being in deep conversation with an admired friend or loved one. Explore your imagination and make notes in your journal about the following questions:

- Charlotte Moss uses three words — *comfort, passion,* and *humor* — to define the values she holds for design. What are at least three words that exemplify the most important values you hold?
- When you think of living an exemplary, satisfying, fulfilling life that is congruent with your values, what does this mean for you?
- What qualities do you want in the following areas of your

life: physical health; relationships with friends, loved ones, and business associates; emotional well-being; financial circumstances; professional endeavors; home and work environments; intellectual growth; entertainment; and spirituality (however you might define it)?

- What will you need to change, continue, or develop in your relationship with money in order to support living the quality of life you want?

- What resources, support, information, or inspiration will you need in order to create or maintain these qualities in your life?

As many people define it, living sterling money behavior means that every transaction — how money comes to them, how they spend it, how they share it, and how they save it — should reflect the self-respect and financial integrity that they continue to learn and toward which they strive. They seek to live in authenticity, balancing their most deeply held values and their money behaviors. (At least most of the time. We're all works in progress, and when we're stressed or overwhelmed, old fears and behaviors can resurface.) This means that they're free to create the comforts, pleasures, and experiences that they find satisfying, without guilt or shame. It means that they can be generous while still honoring their needs and limits. It means that they're free of obsession and worry about money, but that they will remain clear and conscious about how they deal with it.

> *People are like stained-glass windows. They sparkle and shine when the sun is out, but when darkness sets in, their true beauty is revealed only if there is a light from within.*
>
> — ELISABETH KÜBLER-ROSS

This is real financial health. This is how I want to live. It's how you deserve to live too.

My Hopes for You

It's up to you, just as it was up to me, to heal your relationship with money. It will not always be easy, but what you will gain along the way will be worth every effort.

The progression from shaky to stable and from stable to sterling is the path of Financial Recovery in a nutshell. Money does not have to be a source of crisis, pain, fear, shame, or distraction. Instead, by applying some simple strategies with courage and commitment, you can transform it into a vital tool that can help you live in a deeply satisfying, fulfilling, and expansive way.

The journey of Financial Recovery requires commitment and an investment of your time, energy, and money. It will involve facing your fears and tapping into your strengths to deepen them. There is a bridge in front of you. It may at first be cloaked in fog. It may appear shaky and unstable. But it is, nonetheless, a bridge.

You are worth the investment it takes to cross that bridge. You deserve a life in which your needs are met and your future is secure.

I hope that the information and stories in this book provide you with both the tools and the inspiration you need to begin and continue on your journey to financial health and well-being. Beyond that, I hope the financial life you design serves you in every aspect of your life, bringing you satisfaction, pleasure, and growth.

I invite you to join me and many others as we continue to walk across the bridge from where we are to where we want to be in our relationships with money. You too will experience the power, joy, and hopefulness that come with having a healthy relationship with money. I invite you to transform money from an obstacle into a powerful tool that helps you claim the satisfying life you were meant to live.

Appreciations

*I*f it takes a village to raise a child, it seems that it takes at least that to write and publish a book.

I'd like to thank the amazing people at New World Library (NWL). Publisher Marc Allen brought me the unexpected opportunity to assemble the ideas and experiences of my life's work into book form and reassured me by saying, "Just talk about what you do." Georgia Hughes provided the initial support during the early phase, when I was just figuring out what to do. I appreciate her strong backbone and encouragement. I can't believe my good fortune to have landed in the gifted hands of NWL's managing editor, Kristen Cashman, whose gentle, patient, and expert guidance helped to bring the work to final form. Publicity director Monique Muhlenkamp's expertise is already proving invaluable for getting this work into the hands of real people who need it.

Everyone needs a personal champion, and I found mine in John Glover. John, you were there when Financial Recovery was in its infancy and have been so much a part of watching it grow, develop, and mature into what it is today. The value of your brilliant mind, your open heart, and your enormous capacity for supporting me are immeasurable. Words cannot convey my gratitude to you — for everything.

Of all the people who helped on this book, no one has done more or been more dedicated than Betsy Graziani Fasbinder. Day after day, month after month, you worked with me to craft this book into what I hope is an inspirational and moving work. I so appreciate your unfailing talent, good spirits, and dedication. To you go my deepest thanks for helping me bring my life's work to the printed page.

I hold a special and deep gratitude for my dear friend and colleague Mikelann Valterra. Mikelann, I appreciate you every day for your talent, creativity, and dedication. But now I have an even richer gratitude for your loyalty, passion, and support. For fifteen years, you've "had my back," and I count you among my most valuable of treasures. I could not cherish you more if you were my own daughter.

To Frances and Vincent Kreizenbeck — my Aunt Fran and Uncle Binnie — to whom this book is dedicated: You took me in when I needed someone most, loved me, fed me, nurtured me, and gave me a sense of family. The riches you gave me were so much more valuable than money.

To my sister-cousin, Sandy Jones, I thank you for your willingness to listen with an open heart and provide emotional support beyond measure — not just in the writing of this book but in the lifetime we've shared together. With fine-tooth comb at the ready, you labored over sentences with the dedication and commitment for which I've always admired you. Kent Jones, I thank you for your professorial eye and your insightful side comments, which helped so much along the way.

If I could choose my sisters, Barbara Stanny would be among them. Barbara, you have not only shared your friendship with me for many years but also opened your beautiful guest home to me when I needed to escape and reflect as I worked on this project. Colleague, friend, and sister — Barbara, you are all of these to me.

Many skilled helping professionals agreed to be interviewed

for this book. For their time, professional wisdom, and insights
— as well as friendship — I thank Mary Beth McClure, MFT;
Danielle Ray, MFT; David Krueger, MD; Kip Flock, LCSW;
Pamela Ableidinger, PhD; Jyotika Vazirani, CRNP, CNS; Kathy
Fahmie, LCSW; Judith Flory, LCSW; Gerri Detweiler; Norton
Tooby; and Kathleen Mitchell, PhD, who was so instrumental as
a career counselor.

Special thanks to John Bradshaw for not only writing the
foreword but being such an inspiration for so many years. Your
pioneering work on the topic of shame has provided healing to
countless people. For your kindness and generosity, I am truly
grateful.

Heartfelt thanks to Tom Johnson, Beverly Flood, John L.
Levy, and Chris Windiel. Theo Gund, you took me under your
wing when I first started this work. Thank you for your belief in
me. Lynne Elliot-Harding, you're more than a friend, more than
a colleague. You were among the first people to hear about my
business dreams for what Financial Recovery could become. You
believed in me and supported me in more ways than I thought
possible.

Anne Marie Ferguson, you take on tasks big and small and
execute them with excellence and grace. What you do for me and
the Financial Recovery Institute goes far beyond your job de-
scription as "executive virtual assistant." Our pace may not allow
me to tell you often enough that I appreciate all you do.

Many Financial Recovery clients agreed to let me share their
stories in this book. While names, identities, and geographical
details were changed to protect their privacy, I have done my best
to render the essential truths of their stories as best I could. I
am grateful to you all for your candor and your trust. I know in
my heart that your stories will resonate with readers and provide

them with inspiration to take their own first steps. Special appreciation goes to Catherine and Michael, who allowed me to share so many details of their journey in order to help others. You are the poster children for what Financial Recovery can mean as a transformative experience. You continue to teach and inspire me.

Literally hundreds of clients and dozens of Financial Recovery counselors and trainees over the years have been my most invaluable teachers. You have all taught me how to develop and fine-tune this process so that it can touch and transform people's lives, and that transformation will now ripple out to the readers of this book. Seeing you learn these principles and then teach them to others has become the manifestation of a dream I've had for a long time. Thank you, thank you.

Over the many years of my own healing path, I've benefited from the skills of several gifted therapists and mentors. Each has supported me as I've excavated the more painful memories of my own history and encouraged me as I've rejected deep feelings of shame and embraced hope and health. They have reminded me of my worth and helped me recognize that I could take care of myself. These teachers have been an invaluable part of my learning process, and I am truly grateful.

If family love could be measured in dollars, I'd be a multibillionaire. My daughters, Terri de Langis and Tammie Mansuy, of course I love you, but you are also amazing women who inspire me every day by living lives of your own design. My stepsons, Mike and Ian Glover, I hold both of you so close to my heart. Ian, I admire the way you stay true to what you love and bring joy to so many. Mike, I appreciate your ability to always come up with a solution. To my sons-in-law, Mark de Langis and Mike Mansuy, I trust each of you implicitly and appreciate how much of a rock you have each been in my and my daughters' lives. You both, along with Mike Glover's beautiful wife, Laura, have been key in giving me the best gift possible by creating loving and nurturing homes for your children. What more could a grandmother ask for?

"Proud grandmother" doesn't begin to describe how I feel about Mathieu, Nicholas, Christopher, Jacqueline, and little Addison. Watching each of you as you discover your passions and your individual way in the world is such a source of joy for me that I cannot possibly measure it.

To all my family members, dear friends, and loved ones, I've missed you as I've devoted so much time to creating this book. I thank you all for your patience. I look forward to more leisurely times of enjoying your company. I'm opening my calendar now. I love you all.

Notes

INTRODUCTION
The Bridge to a Healthy Relationship with Money

1. Robert H. Schuller, *Move Ahead with Possibility Thinking*, audiocassettes (New York: Doubleday, 1967).

CHAPTER 1
Understanding Your Relationship with Money

1. David Krueger and John David Mann, *The Secret Language of Money: How to Make Smarter Financial Decisions and Live a Richer Life* (New York: McGraw-Hill, 2009), p. 77.
2. Mikelann Valterra, personal communication to author.
3. Quoted in Oprah Winfrey, *Oprah Winfrey Speaks* (New York: Wiley, 1998), p. 132.
4. *Merriam-Webster's Ninth New Collegiate Dictionary* (Springfield, MA: Merriam-Webster, 1983).

CHAPTER 2
Déjà Vu All Over Again

1. Barbara Stanny, *Overcoming Underearning* (New York: HarperCollins, 2005), p. 3.
2. Ted Klontz, Rick Kahler, and Brad Klontz, *The Financial Wisdom of Ebenezer Scrooge: 5 Principles to Transform Your Relationship with Money* (Deerfield Beach, FL: Health Communications, Inc., 2006), p. 4.

CHAPTER 3

Healing the Wounds of Shame and Deprivation

1. John Bradshaw, *Healing the Shame That Binds You* (Deerfield Beach, FL: Health Communications, 1988), p. 71.
2. Abraham H. Maslow, "A Theory of Human Motivation," *Psychological Review* 50(4), 1943, pp. 370–96.

CHAPTER 4

Getting on Track

1. Mikelann Valterra, "Practice 'Radical Financial Clarity,'" *Daily Worth*, October 21, 2009. www.dailyworth.com/blog/276-practice-radical -financial-clarity.
2. Mikelann Valterra, *Why Women Earn Less: How to Make What You're Really Worth* (Franklin Lakes, NJ: Career Press, 2004).

CHAPTER 6

Saving Your Way Out of Debt

1. *60 Minutes*, "The Power of Plastic," January 23, 2001, http://www.cbsnews .com/stories/2001/01/19/60II/main265630.shtml (accessed January 4, 2011).

CHAPTER 8

Imagining Sterling Money Behaviors

1. Charlotte Moss, *A Passion for Detail* (New York: Doubleday, 1991), p. 99.

More Support for Your
Financial Recovery Process

Some people can read a book, learn what's in its pages, and put it right into practice. This book gives you resources, strategies, and inspiration to make Financial Recovery a reality in your life, but I know that many of us (including me and many of my clients over the years) need more than just a book to implement real changes in our lives. We need support, guidance, encouragement, and the inspiration that others can provide. You might find the following resources helpful as you cross your own bridge to a financially abundant and healthy life.

DEBTORS' ANONYMOUS (DA) is a free self-help program available in nearly every community and by phone for those in very remote locations. This 12-step program allows its members to support and inspire one another in a nonjudgmental way. You can find information about DA by doing a simple internet search or looking in your local telephone directory.

I created THE FINANCIAL RECOVERY INSTITUTE to train counselors to work with clients who struggle in their relationship with money. To find a certified Financial Recovery counselor who can help you apply the principles and practices found in this book, go to www.financialrecovery.com. The website also offers:

• Free downloadable articles, resources, and information to support your Financial Recovery

- Information about purchasing MoneyMinder products, including personal and business money management software and the *MoneyMinder Personal Autobiography* workbook.
- A free subscription to my blog, which offers updates and inspiration for keeping on track.

Index

instant gratification, 81–82
insurance expenses, 131, 168, 194
interest, 55, 111, 202
Internal Revenue Service (IRS),
  56
internet shopping, 52–53, 99
investments, 131, 188, 203–5
IRAs, 203–4, 205

J

Jackson, Michael, 38
James (case study), 221–22
Joanna (case study), 218–19
jobs
  changing, 222–23, 234–35
  leaving, 201
  past, inventory of, 213–16
  salaried, 234–35
Joe (case study), 17–18
Josh (case study), 49–51
journal. *See* money journal
Joyce, James, 156
Julia (case study), 19

K

Kafka, Franz, 89
Kahler, Rick, 48
Klontz, Brad, 48
Klontz, Ted, 48
Krueger, David, 21
Kübler-Ross, Elisabeth, 251
Kupferberg, Tuli, 37

L

late fees, 55, 111, 147
leisure time, 111

Lewis, C.S., 69
lifestyle, and spending plans,
  167–68
Lila (case study), 33–35
living expansively, 13
loans
  debt and, 173
  Money/Life Drain and, 40
  payment of, 111
Lorimer, George, 97
Lydia (case study), 52–53

M

Maggie (case study), 46–47
making do, 71–72, 76, 92
Marilyn (case study), 70–71
Maslow, Abraham, Hierarchy of
  Human Needs, 77–79, *78*, 85,
  129, 184
McClure, Mary Beth, 67
McGraw, Phil, 103
Melanie (case study), 42–43, 205
memory, and tracking, 116–17
Mexico, Gulf of, oil spill in (2010),
  66
Michael (case study), 226–29
money
  consciousness of/connection
    with, 29, 97, 239
  "enough," 247–48
  meaning attributed to, 20–21
  "not enough," 20, 247
  secrecy about, 103–5
  work and, 12, 207
money behaviors
  deprivation as cause of, 61–63
  sterling, 13, 248–51

About the Author

*K*aren McCall developed the highly acclaimed Financial Recovery process after she struggled for years to heal her own crippling relationship with money. In 1988 she created Financial Recovery, and ten years later she founded the Financial Recovery Institute, which trains and certifies mental-healthcare professionals and entrepreneurs to use the counseling processes and practical tools of Financial Recovery to help people transform their relationship with money and create lifelong financial well-being.

A nationally recognized speaker and financial expert, Karen has been quoted in publications such as *Entrepreneur, Money* magazine, *Kiplinger's Personal Finance, Bottom Line, Women's Day, Working Mother,* and *USA Weekend.* She is the author of *It's Your Money: Achieving Financial Well-Being,* a contributor to *I Shop, Therefore I Am: Compulsive Buying and the Search for Self* (edited by April Lane Benson), and the creator of several MoneyMinder® software products. Karen lives in Sonoma County, California, where she spends her limited spare time gardening and spoiling her grandchildren.

HELPING TO PRESERVE OUR ENVIRONMENT

7,205 trees were saved

New World Library uses 100% postconsumer-waste recycled paper for our books whenever possible, even if it costs more. During 2009 this choice saved the following precious resources:

	ENERGY	WASTEWATER	GREENHOUSE GASES	SOLID WASTE
	22 MILLION BTU	3 MILLION GAL.	685,000 LB.	200,000 LB.

Environmental impact estimates were made using the Environmental Defense Fund Paper Calculator @ www.papercalculator.org.